Better Homes and Gardens®

NEEDLEPOINT

BETTER HOMES AND GARDENS ® BOOKS

Editor: Gerald Knox
Art Director: Ernest Shelton
Associate Art Director: Randall Yontz
Production and Copy Editors: David Kirchner, Paul S. Kitzke
Crafts Editor: Nancy Lindemeyer
Senior Crafts Editor — Books: Joan Cravens
Associate Crafts Editor: Ann Levine
Senior Graphic Designer: Harijs Priekulis
Graphic Designers: Sheryl Veenschoten, Faith Berven, Rich Lewis,
Neoma Alt West, Linda Ford

CONTENTS

Needlepoint is such an exciting craft that even beginning stitchers can have fun and enjoy fabulous results with it. To prove it, here is a section of designs with the beginner in mind. Advanced needlepointers will also enjoy these excellent quick-to-stitch patterns that are lovely to look at.

Needlepoint
An Exciting and Elegant Craft_____ 4-23

Pillows, pillows everywhere – each a different style or design and each a different combination of colors and stitches. If you fancy the idea of learning lots of techniques on one piece of canvas, pick one of these easy-to-stitch pillows and start right in. You'll learn many valuable needlepoint tips along the way.

Pillows
A Primer of Design and Pattern_____ 24-39

Are you ready for an adventure? If so, browse through this section of out-of-the-ordinary needlepoint ideas. You'll find projects a creative stitcher will treasure. If some of the techniques seem a bit unusual, don't worry – step-by-step directions are included.

Adventures in Needlepoint
Unique Projects to Stitch_____ 40-57

Creative Techniques
New Ways with Needlepoint _____ **58-71**

Unusual techniques and materials can make your needlepoint extraordinary. Stitch with string, for example, and needlepoint becomes a new craft. Metal threads, inlaid stones, raffia, sewing thread, and even leftover yarns all present challenges. Find out how to use these materials in this intriguing section of projects.

Spectacular Stitchery
Art from Your Needle _____ **72-92**

Creating intricate patterns and designs is one of the joys of needlepoint. These projects use yarn on canvas the same way an artist uses paint. The result is a very special, very lovely piece of needlework to enjoy forever.

Needlepoint

An Exciting and Elegant Craft

Needlepoint is one of our most popular needle arts. And no wonder—since this exciting and creative craft is not only easy to master, but also offers so many techniques and materials to inspire you. You can work everything from minute stitches on fine-mesh canvas to quick-and-easy quickpoint rugs; from smooth, flat stitches to magnificently textured ones; and from delicate pictorial designs to bold, splashy geometrics. And in this book, you'll find beautiful and imaginative projects that illustrate just how varied and rewarding needlepoint can be. This first section, for example, includes quickpoint and other simple-to-stitch projects like the rug and pillows shown here. For complete instructions, please turn to page 21.

Needlepoint Basics

Crafting beautiful fabric is what needlepoint is all about. Needlepoint is a form of embroidery on canvas in which the stitches cover the background fabric completely, creating an exciting new fabric from the basic materials of stitchery. And while design is important, an understanding of materials and techniques also is essential to successful completion of a needlepoint project.

Here's what you need to know to get started. When you're ready to begin stitching, please turn the page for stitchery tips.

Needlepoint Canvas

Needlepoint canvas is a sturdy, open-weave fabric that is used as a framework for the stitches that are worked into it. It is available in several weaves and a large number of widths, and it is sized according to the number of vertical threads per inch; the larger the number of threads per inch, the smaller the actual stitches will be.

Mono canvas, shown at left, is made with single threads woven together in a plain over-and-under weave so each mesh, or space between threads, is the same size. It is available in #10-, #12-, #14-, #16-, #18-, #20-, and #24-count sizes (threads per inch).

Penelope canvas is made with *double* threads, as shown at right. It's a strong canvas that can be used for regular stitches that cover the double threads (gros point) or for fine stitches worked into the smaller spaces formed by the double threads (petit point).

The most widely used penelope canvas is #10/20-count; the first mesh number indicates threads per inch for gros point and the second indicates threads per inch for petit point. It can also be found in #11/22-count and #12/24-count sizes, and is available in #3½-, #4-, #5-, and #7-count sizes for rugs and other quickpoint projects.

Interlock canvas, shown at right, is a locked-weave canvas also made with double threads. Warp threads are twisted between each pair of weft threads, making this canvas resistant to raveling and distortion from the pull of the stitches.

Because of the way they're woven, the threads of interlock canvas cannot be separated for petit point, but they're easy to

see through and paint. Interlock canvas is available in sizes ranging from less than three to more than 50 threads per inch.

While canvas is available in linen, nylon, or plastic, the most widely used form is cotton because it's strong and retains its starched body well (linen canvas tends to become limp). Nylon and plastic canvases are durable, but plastic is best for projects that need to be stiff and flat or that have pieces that are cut and pieced together. Nylon is similar to plastic but is more flexible.

Most canvases are white, but some ecru, tan, and peach shades also are available. And cotton and linen canvases are easily dyed.

Judging Quality in Canvas

For a genuinely beautiful and long-lasting piece of needlepoint, use the best materials you can afford. Here are a few pointers for judging quality.

First, be sure the canvas is woven of long, smooth threads. Spaces between threads should be clear rather than full of fuzz or hairs from warp and weft threads. Also look for canvas that is free of knots and weak-looking or broken threads.

The weave should be uniform, with an equal number of warp and weft threads per inch. Warp threads and selvages should be straight, crossing weft threads at right angles. If the weave is crooked to begin with, it's apt to be crooked even after blocking.

Yarns and Threads

The sky's the limit when choosing yarns and threads for needlepoint, as long as you can thread the fiber you've selected through the eye of a needle. Don't hesitate to use wool, cotton, linen, and silk yarns, as

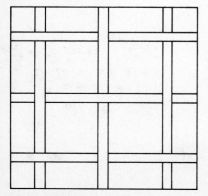

Mono canvas

well as metallic threads, macrame cords, ribbons, and even fabric strips for special effects!

Wool is the most popular yarn for traditional needlepoint, however. Of the many types available, *Persian wool* is the most widely used because it wears well, is easy to work with, and is available in over 300 colors. Each strand of Persian wool is made of three plies loosely twisted together so they can be separated and used individually.

Nantucket wool, which comes in tightly twisted four-ply strands, is comparable to a two-ply strand of Persian wool. Long fibers give this yarn a texture similar to tapestry yarn.

Tapestry wool comes in four-ply strands. It's a strong, smooth yarn available in a wide variety of lot-dyed colors so you can be sure colors are consistent, which makes it an excellent yarn for stitching backgrounds.

Crewel wool, used for embroidery, is a fine yarn that's especially nice for petit point. It comes in one-, three-, and five-ply sizes.

When purchasing yarn, try to buy enough for the entire project so you can be sure colors match. Also, look for colorfast yarns so you don't ruin a beautiful piece of handwork in the blocking stage.

If yarns are not colorfast, rinse dye residues from them by soaking them in lukewarm water while they're still wrapped in skeins. Let them dry thoroughly before you begin stitching.

Needles and Other Tools

For stitching needlepoint, use tapestry needles with blunt tips and large, elongated eyes. They'll help you avoid splitting the yarns or threads of the canvas and won't put undue stress on the yarn in the needle. The needle should be large enough to hold the thread easily, but small enough to pass through the mesh on the canvas without distorting the threads.

Check the chart at right for the needle to fit your canvas.

Equipment needed in addition to needles includes scissors with sharp, narrow points for snipping out mistakes; an emery-stuffed pincushion for polishing needles; masking tape; and a yarn caddy, if desired.

Frames

Many needlepointers mount their canvases in a frame for working, freeing both hands for stitching (with one hand atop the canvas and the other beneath it). This often results in a more even tension, which minimizes distortion of the canvas during stitching and reduces the need for blocking. Also, large projects are frequently worked more easily on a frame than in your lap.

There are several types of frames available. A scroll or slate frame is the most commonly used type because it's adjustable and is available in several sizes. To use one, attach canvas to rollers at the top and bottom and lace it to the sides, as shown at right. (Make sure the grain of the canvas is straight as you attach it to the frame.) The rollers turn the canvas so you can work the design one section at a time.

Mount the frame on a floor stand or prop it against a table to free your hands for stitching.

To make your own frame, assemble artist's stretcher strips into a frame at least one inch larger on all sides than your project. Staple canvas to the frame with grain lines straight.

If you wish to work in your lap, roll the canvas rather than folding it to avoid breaking the sizing. Roll it around a cardboard tube (from paper towels) and secure the ends with paper clips.

continued

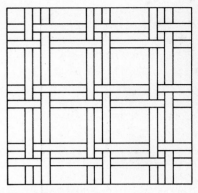

Penelope canvas

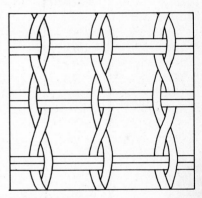

Interlock canvas

Canvas size	Needle size
#3½, #4, #5	#13
#7	#15
#10	#18
#12	#20
#14, #16	#22
#18, #20, #24	#22

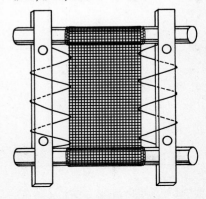

Mount canvas in a frame

Needlepoint Basics *(continued)*

Beautiful stitchery begins before the needle ever enters the canvas, with the careful handling and preparation of canvas and yarns. For directions for transferring designs to canvas and preparing it for needlepoint, see pages 10 and 42. And following are some tips for working with yarn and making the stitches that will start you off to successful stitching.

After completing your needlepoint, block it to restore the canvas to its original shape and to prepare it for final finishing.

Working with the Grain of the Yarn

Yarn, like fabric, has "grain." If you run a piece of wool through your fingers or across your cheek, you'll notice that it is smoother in one direction than the other. And when dividing strands of cotton embroidery floss, you'll find they separate fairly easily in one direction, but get hopelessly tangled in the other! If you thread the needle so you stitch "with the grain," working the thread in its smoother direction, the yarn will remain springy and attractive-looking longer than if you stitch "against the grain."

Cutting Yarn into Short Lengths

Cutting yarn into short lengths also prevents it from looking worn and tired from being pulled through the canvas too often. Cut floss or cotton pearl about 36 inches long and wool strands about 18 inches long. Silk and metallic threads should be cut to even shorter lengths.

Separating Strands into Plies

Next, separate strands into individual plies, if necessary. Then put plies back together again before threading the needle. This minimizes the amount of twist in the yarn so stitches cover the canvas better and are smoother and flatter.

While the number of plies used for a stitch depends on the size of the canvas, it's also influenced by the direction of the stitches. Diagonal stitches, such as tent stitches, lie directly over an intersection of threads. Straight stitches, such as bargello stitches, lie between threads and may require additional plies to cover the canvas adequately. So if necessary, plan to use one or more additional plies in the needle for straight stitches than for diagonal ones.

Stitching without Knots

Knots tied on the back of the canvas are apt to cause unsightly bumps. To avoid them, weave ends of yarn into the back of the work, or begin and end with waste knots. To make a waste knot, knot end of yarn and insert needle into canvas from front to back, so knot is on top. Then stitch over thread end, securing it. Clip knot and pull end of yarn to the back.

Working the Stitches

If you are a beginning needlepointer — or an experienced one learning a new stitch — keep scrap canvas handy to practice on. The time spent mastering a new stitch will be amply rewarded once you switch to your actual project canvas. The tension on the stitches will be more uniform once you've mastered the technique, and you'll spend less time picking out inaccurate or unattractive stitches.

To avoid splitting and damaging stitches already worked, whenever possible stitch "from empty to full": bring the needle up from the back of the canvas to the front, in an empty mesh; then take it down, from front to back, in a mesh that already has another stitch in it — a full one.

As you stitch, maintain even tension on the thread from stitch to stitch and with every motion needed to make a single stitch. If you pull the yarn too tight, it will not cover the canvas completely. When worked too loose, yarn tends to snag easily. With uniform tension, the stitches will look better and you'll be less apt to distort the canvas.

Finally, it's easiest to stitch a design with separate needles threaded with yarn in each color. When working with several needles, however, don't carry the yarn more than a few meshes across the back of the canvas.

Instead, weave thread through the backs of the stitches already worked. Or weave the thread end into the back, clip it, and start fresh in the new location.

Stitching with the Grain of the Canvas

Stitching with the grain of the canvas reduces tension on the threads and the degree of distortion of the canvas, which makes blocking easier. Stitches also cover canvas better than if they're worked against the grain.

This technique is particularly important on backgrounds, since they form a large part of most needlepoint designs. And the best background stitch, which distorts canvas the least, is probably the basket-weave stitch. To work it with the grain, you need to examine the canvas before you begin stitching. (For basic stitch how-to, see the Glossary.)

To determine whether the first row of basket-weave stitches should be worked from right to left or from left to right, observe the cross of canvas threads that the first stitch will cover. If the vertical (warp) thread is on top, work the needle vertically, point down, from the top left stitch in the row. The row will run downhill from upper left to lower right.

If the horizontal (weft) thread is on top, work the needle horizontally, with the point to the left, from the bottom right stitch in the row. The row will run uphill from right to left.

Blocking Needlepoint Canvas

After stitching your needlepoint, return the canvas to its original shape by blocking it on a firm, flat surface. A good blocking job

eliminates the distortion that occurs from the tension and pull of the stitches.

If you've worked in basket-weave stitches, which greatly reduce distortion, you may need only to steam-press the back of the canvas to restore its shape.

A design worked entirely in continental stitches, however, may be very distorted and need two or three blockings before it returns to its original shape. Here is an explanation of the correct procedure for blocking your needlepoint canvases.

Sprinkle the canvas with water until the yarn feels damp (but not drenched) on both sides. Or, wet a clean towel, wring it out, and leave the canvas wrapped inside the damp towel for several hours or overnight.

Tack the damp needlepoint facedown to a blocking board made of clean, ½-inch plywood or pine boards. (Be sure to use rustproof thumbtacks or push pins.) Make sure the blocking board is larger than the needlepoint piece and has straight edges. To help line up the edges, cover the board with gingham fabric and use the checks as a guide for squaring canvas, or mark it with a 1-inch grid drawn with a *waterproof* marking pen.

When tacking the canvas to the board, start in corner A, as shown in the diagram at right, and gradually move down sides AB and AD, placing the tacks one inch apart. Make sure the canvas is flush with the blocking board so the edges are straight. Then continue along sides BC and CD, ending in corner C. Pull the canvas taut as you go, making sure the edges are straight and aligned with the gingham checks or the 1-inch grid.

Sprinkle canvas with water again and let it dry thoroughly —at least 24 hours— before removing from the board.

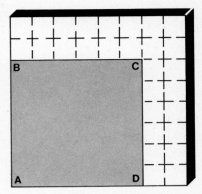

Mount canvas on a blocking board

Quickpoint Rose Wreath

With needlepoint, you can enjoy the beauty of roses year 'round. This quickpoint wreath is worked in wool rug yarns, mounted on plywood, and framed. Because of the large-mesh canvas, progress is fast, especially since you use only two basic stitches – continental and basket-weave. Secure the canvas to a needlepoint frame while you work to prevent distortion.

The pattern and a closeup view of the wreath are on pages 12 and 13.

Materials
26x26 inches #5-count rug
  canvas
¾ pound white rug yarn (see
  note at right)
Approximately 15 yards rug
  yarn in each of the following
  colors: red, pink, and green
  (see note at right)
#13 tapestry needle
Masking tape
Needlepoint frame or four
  26-inch artist's stretcher
  strips
Quilt batting
28x28x⅜-inch piece of
  plywood
10 feet of 1x3-inch pine
White paint

Directions
Note: We used Paternayan rug yarns for this wreath; the specific color numbers are noted on the chart on page 12. Other rug yarns of comparable weight and color may be substituted, however.

Bind the raw edges of the canvas with masking tape to prevent fraying. Then mount the canvas on a needlepoint frame or on artist's stretcher strips to prevent distortion as you work.

Because yarn sometimes contains color residue that runs when the needlework is blocked or cleaned, soak it for a few minutes in cool water. Then let it dry thoroughly before beginning to stitch.

Mark the center of the canvas and begin stitching there, following the chart on the next page. Work the roses first, and then the leaves, using continental stitches. Finally, work the background in the center of the wreath and around the roses until the square measures 23½x23½ inches. Use either continental stitches or basket-weave stitches for the background.

Cut two layers of quilt batting the exact size of the finished wreath. Center the batting and the canvas on the plywood board without cutting or turning the canvas; staple the canvas in place.

Notch *the edges* of the pine boards to the thickness of the plywood (about ⅜ inch), cut and miter the boards to fit the plywood, and glue and nail the frame together. Paint it white. Mount the plywood in the frame by tacking it in place with wire brads.

continued

Transferring a Design to Canvas

Enlarge or reduce your pattern to size on brown wrapping paper or white craft paper, following the directions on page 42. Then go over the outlines with a black marking pen so they are easy to see. Next, tape the pattern to a large, flat surface and cover it with a sheet of clear plastic or acetate to keep it clean, if desired. Center the canvas on top of the pattern and secure it with masking tape. Be sure to leave at least two inches of canvas on each side of the design for blocking and finishing.

Using a light-colored waterproof pen, transfer the pattern to the canvas. To be sure the pen is waterproof, test it by marking on a sample piece of canvas and sprinkling the canvas with water. If the lines don't run or bleed, the pen is safe to use. It is important to use a light-colored pen so the lines do not show through the stitching once you work the canvas. Transfer the entire design to the canvas by tracing over the pattern, following the lines carefully. This technique gives you a basic pattern outline that is adequate when working a simple design with easy-to-read lines and shapes.

If your pattern is more complicated or requires intricate shading, it's a good idea to paint your canvas with acrylic or oil paints, as explained on page 43. This assures you of getting all the details and shading shown on the original pattern. Another way to work a needlepoint pattern, especially when only a portion of it is given, is to chart the entire design on graph paper with symbols or colored pencils and work directly from the chart onto canvas.

Quickpoint Rose Wreath *(continued)*

Color Key

Symbol	Color
■	# 818 dark red
◪	#848 med. dark red
⊠	# 858 med. red
◨	# 868 light red
⊡	#878 pink
◉	#505 dark green
◎	#510 med. dark green
▣	#555 med. light green
⊞	#570 light green
☐	#010 white

Easy-to-Stitch Bargello Bench

Wonderfully quick, easy, and versatile, bargello is satin stitching on canvas. Traditionally, it is worked over four threads in a "dome-and-spires" or "flame-stitch" design. The pattern is established with the first line of stitches across the canvas, and all subsequent rows duplicate it exactly. And by varying yarns and colors, the effect can be dramatic, as in the bench cover opposite, or subtle, as in the pillow on page 65.

Materials

10 shades of 3-ply Persian yarn
   (see note below)
21x31 inches #12-count
   interlock canvas, or sufficient
   canvas to fit your own bench
   (be sure to add 2-inch
   margins to each side)
#18 tapestry needle
Needlepoint frame (optional)
Masking tape
Quilt batting
⅜x15x23-inch plywood board,
   or size to fit your bench
Staple gun

Directions

Note: This bargello pattern uses five shades each in two different colors of yarn. Use four 32-inch strands of yarn of each shade (approximately 3½ yards) to make the 17x27-inch cover shown.

To adjust the yarn quantities to fit your bench, stitch one complete row of the design. Determine how much yarn you have used for the row and then determine how many rows you will need to complete the design. Do this by counting the number of meshes in the length of the finished design and dividing by four (since each stitch covers four threads of canvas).

If you need to adjust the width of the rows, work one row starting in the center of the row and working out to one side. Stop the design wherever necessary, or continue the design if the rows need to be longer. To continue the design, pick up a portion of the design from the pattern below and stitch that extra portion on both sides of the canvas (so the design remains symmetrical).

Tape the edges of the canvas to prevent raveling. With a waterproof pen, mark a 2-inch border on the canvas to be left unstitched. Attach the canvas to a scroll frame, if desired, to minimize distortion from the stitching and to reduce the need for blocking when the needlepoint is finished.

Begin stitching with the lightest shade of one color. Following the chart below, begin the first horizontal row on the left-hand side of the canvas and work to the center. Then, reverse the pattern shown in the chart below and complete the row by stitching to the right-hand side of the canvas.

Complete four more rows, one on top of the other, using each shade of the first color. Work the rows according to shade, going from light to dark. Then begin a sixth row, using the lightest shade of the second color. Complete the next four rows as for the first color, going from light to dark so each shade is used once.

These first ten rows make up the pattern repeat. Continue working this repeat until you reach 27 inches, or the desired length.

To finish the two ends, fill in the pattern between the peaks using the correct color sequence so rows are even across ends.

Block the canvas, following the directions on page 9. Cut three to five 15x23-inch pieces of quilt batting and layer them on top of the plywood. Cover the batting with the finished bargello and staple the 2-inch margins to the back of the board.

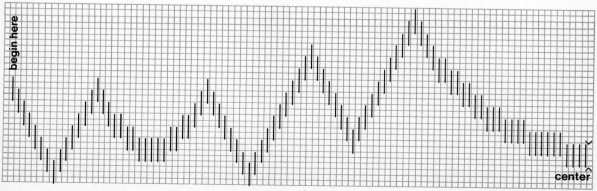

begin here

center

1 Square = 1 Mesh

Easy-to-Stitch Apple Picture

A celebration of the growth of a seed, our 12-inch needlepoint picture, opposite, is worked entirely in basket-weave and continental stitches. And the individual shapes are large enough to keep the overall design simple and easy to follow.

When the needlepoint is complete, cut a piece of cardboard the size of the finished design, tape the canvas around it, and mount the picture in a frame.

Materials

15x15 inches #12-count canvas
40-yard skeins Elsa Williams wool tapestry yarn, or any similar substitute, in the following amounts and colors: 2 #N801 black, 2 #N302 bronze, 2 #N213 orange, 2 #N211 red, 1 #N402 green, 1 #N600 purple, and 1 #N805 off-white
#18 tapestry needle
Masking tape
Waterproof marking pen
Needlepoint frame (optional)
12x12 inches cardboard
12-inch-square picture frame

Color Key

B   Black
BR Bronze
O   Orange
R   Red
G   Green
P   Purple
W Off-white

Directions

Bind the edges of the canvas with masking tape, and with a waterproof pen, mark a 137-mesh-square block in the center of the canvas. Using the graph below, transfer the pattern to the canvas following the directions on page 10. If you wish to paint the design on the canvas, see page 43.

If desired, mount the canvas in a needlepoint frame to minimize distortion and to reduce the necessity for blocking. Cut the yarn into 18-inch lengths for working. Following the color key below, outline the large shapes with a row of continental stitches and fill with basket-weave stitches. Outline and fill smaller shapes in continental stitches. (For an explanation of the stitches, see the Glossary on pages 93 to 96.) Begin and end lengths of yarn with waste knots (which are explained in the Glossary) to minimize bulk on the back of the canvas.

When the needlepoint is finished, block the canvas following the directions on page 9. Then trim the cardboard backing, if necessary, to fit the *worked area* of the canvas. Lay the canvas facedown and center the cardboard over it. Pull the unworked canvas over the edge of the cardboard and tape it securely in place, starting in the center of the edge and working toward the sides. Miter the corners, trimming excess canvas to reduce bulk. Mount the needlepoint in a frame.

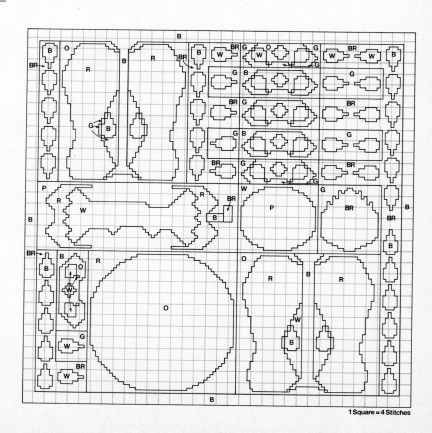

1 Square = 4 Stitches

Quickpoint WELCOME Rug

Large-mesh canvas makes this 27x42-inch WELCOME rug, with its Jacobean-style border, a quick and easy project to stitch. The completely graphed pattern is on page 18, but you may substitute your name or initials in the center of the rug by following the directions below.

Materials

1⅓ yards 36-inch-wide #5-count interlock rug canvas
Wool rug yarn in the following colors and amounts: white (250 yards), dark blue (200 yards), medium blue (50 yards), and light blue (50 yards)
Large tapestry needle
Masking tape
Waterproof marking pen
Graph paper
4 yards 1-inch-wide blue grosgrain ribbon (optional)
4 yards 4-inch-wide rug binding
11 feet 1x2-inch lumber (frame)
Wood glue and nails
Eye hooks and picture wire
Staple gun

Directions

Cut canvas to 31x46 inches to allow a 2-inch margin around the design. Bind the edges of the canvas with masking tape to keep yarn from tearing on them. Then mark the center of the canvas with a waterproof pen by locating the middle horizontal and vertical threads.

The pattern shown on page 20 is for the upper left quadrant of the border design. Work from the chart, or copy the entire design onto graph paper by flopping the pattern to reproduce the stitch sequence for each quarter of the border.

Center the design on the canvas and begin by working the outermost dark blue border in continental stitches. Work the second and third blue borders, the floral motif, and the WELCOME letters in continental stitches. Fill the background in the center of the rug with white basket-weave stitches. (For an explanation of the stitches, see the Glossary on pages 93 to 96.)

Block the completed rug, following the directions on page 9.

To finish the rug, whipstitch the edge of the rug binding securely to the edge of the needlepoint stitches around the edge of the rug. Assemble a 24x42-inch frame with the 1x2-inch lumber, glue, and nails. Then place the rug facedown on a table and center the frame over it. Starting in the middle of each side, pull the margin of the rug to the back of the frame and staple in place. Miter the corners. The edge of the outermost blue border in the design should fall along the front of the frame.

For an attractive finish on the edge of the frame, blindstitch 1-inch-wide blue ribbon in place over the rug binding along the side edges of the frame. Attach eye hooks and wire for hanging.

How to Stitch a Name or Monogram in the Center of the Rug

To stitch your name or monogram in the center of the rug, work the borders and floral motif following the directions above. Then find a suitable alphabet style by looking through needlepoint or embroidery books; transfer the letters to tracing paper. Or, sketch your letters freehand, making sure they will adapt well.

To plan the size of the letters, keep in mind that the center of the rug measures about 72x150 meshes. Allow a margin of four or five meshes at the sides of the letters so they don't run into the border, and about two meshes between letters. Then divide the number of letters in your name or monogram into 140 to determine the *average* number of meshes you'll need for each letter. Use this only as a guide, however, because some letters such as "l" or "i" require less space than others, such as "m" or "w."

Chart the letters on a sheet of five-squares-per-inch graph paper. This makes them full size so you can easily tell whether they'll need to be enlarged or reduced to fit the available space. When you've designed the letters on graph paper and are satisfied that they'll fit attractively in the center of the rug, stitch them in place with continental stitches.

Quickpoint WELCOME Rug *(continued)*

center of
side border

center of →
top border

(Actual dimensions of rug are 42 X 27 inches worked on five-squares-per-inch interlock canvas. Pattern is ¼ of border)

Color Key
⊠ Dark Blue
⊡ Medium Blue
■ Light Blue

Welcome

1 Square = 1 Stitch

Easy-to-Stitch Wildflower Designs *(shown on pages 4 and 5)*

Wildflowers make lovely needlepoint motifs, whether worked into pillows or a rug, as shown on pages 4 and 5, or into a mirror frame, as shown here. The natural beauty of their simple shapes and brilliant colors makes them easily adaptable to canvas.

Patterns for nine wildflower designs are on page 23. To make the pillows, rug, or frame, enlarge the patterns to different sizes and work them on a variety of canvases in easy-to-master continental and basket-weave stitches.

Pillows
Materials
For each pillow:
14x14 inches #10-count penelope canvas
4-ounce skein #505 green Paternayan 3-ply Persian yarn
Small amounts of Persian yarn in colors shown on patterns
#22 tapestry needle
Polyester fiberfill
14x14 inches backing fabric
Waterproof marking pen

Directions
Note: Finished pillows are ten inches square.

Enlarge the patterns on page 23, using a scale of "one square equals 1¼ inches." Trace each design (centered) onto canvas, using a waterproof marking pen and following the directions on page 10. Tape the edges of the canvas to prevent raveling. Mount canvas in a frame for stitching, if desired.

Begin by stitching the flowers, stems, and leaves in continental stitches, referring to the patterns for colors. Work the background in green basket-weave stitches. (Refer to the Glossary on pages 93 to 96 for stitch how-to, if necessary.) Block finished needlepoint following directions on page 9.

To assemble pillows, sew fronts to backs, right sides facing, stitching close to the last row of needlepoint. Leave an opening for turning. Trim seams to within ½ inch; turn right side out. Stuff the pillow and slip-stitch the opening.

continued

Easy-to-Stitch Wildflower Designs *(continued)*

Rug
Materials
2 yards 40-inch-wide #5-count penelope rug canvas

4-ounce skeins of Paternayan rug yarn, or a similar substitute, in the following amounts and colors: 15 #505 green; 10 #005 white; 2 each #545 and #589 green; 3 #569 green; 1 each of #580 and #527 green; #958, #968, #424, and #978 orange; #421 gold; #144 brown; #741 and #731 blue; #662 and #622 violet; #239, #259, and #279 pink; and #483 yellow

2 yards 36-inch-wide burlap

5½ yards rug binding

#13 tapestry needle

Waterproof marking pen

Masking tape

Staple gun and staples

Carpet thread

Directions
Note: The size of the finished rug is 36x62 inches.

Using a scale of "one square equals one inch," enlarge the patterns and trace them onto separate sheets of paper. Bind the edges of the canvas with tape.

Each motif is worked in a 10½-inch square. The white borders are six stitches wide (1¼ inches).

Beginning two inches below the top raw edge of the canvas, mark off the first six rows for the white border, using a waterproof marker. Measure down 10½ inches and mark another six rows. Continue until you've measured six bands (five blocks).

Next, working from the wide (selvage) edge of the canvas and starting 1½ inches from the edge, mark off a band six rows wide. Measure 10½ inches and mark another six rows. Continue until you have four bands. The canvas should be divided into five rows of three blocks each, with each block separated by a six-row border.

Trace one flower in the center of each square, varying the direction so the flowers either face toward or away from the center.

Work flowers first, using continental or basket-weave stitches. Then work white borders, increasing one stitch in each of the last five rows at the corner of each square to achieve the angled-corner effect shown in the photograph on pages 4 and 5. Fill background with dark green yarn, using basket-weave stitches.

To block the rug, follow directions on page 9. Press seam allowance under; tack to back of rug. Stitch rug binding to the raw edges of the canvas, then cut burlap to fit back of rug. Stitch burlap to binding on back.

Mirror Frame
(shown on page 21)

Materials
22x28 inches #10 mono or #10/20 penelope canvas

#18 tapestry needle

Paternayan 3-ply Persian yarn, or a similar substitute, in the following amounts and colors: 3 ounces each of #010 white and #505 green; 25 yards each of #G64, #545, and #589 green; and 5 yards each of colors indicated on patterns

Waterproof marking pen

½-inch plywood frame to fit finished canvas

14 feet of ½-inch half-round molding to fit edges of frame

Green paint to match background

Mirror to fit inside frame

Brackets

Staple gun and staples

White glue

Directions
Note: The finished size of the frame is 16½x23 inches.

Enlarge the patterns so each square equals ⅓ inch, and trace the patterns onto separate sheets of paper. Bind edges of canvas with masking tape.

Draw the frame on the canvas as follows. Two inches above the lower edge of the canvas, mark off three rows of threads for the first white border. Leaving a two-inch margin along the left side, mark a similar three-row-wide border. Beginning in the lower left corner of the frame, mark one 2¾-inch square and one three-row-wide border; continue across the bottom of canvas until there are five squares divided and bordered with six rows of three-row-wide borders.

Mark the top edge of the bottom frame border (see photograph on page 21). Then, working up the left side of the frame, mark seven 2¾-inch squares divided by borders. Repeat for right side and top.

Following the directions on page 10, trace one wildflower motif onto each square, centering the flowers. Vary the placement of the flowers as shown in the photograph. Work flowers first, using a half cross-stitch. Then fill borders and background with half cross-stitches or continental stitches. When working borders, increase one stitch in each of the last three rows at the corner of each square to achieve the angled-corner effect shown in the photograph.

Block the finished canvas, following the directions on page 9. Then cut a plywood frame to fit behind the needlepoint (cut out the center).

Trim unworked canvas so the edges can be turned under

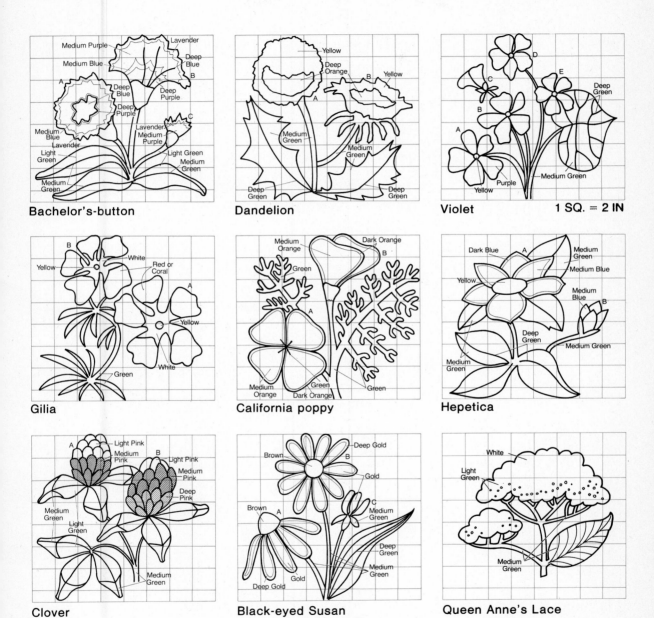

Bachelor's-button

Dandelion

Violet

1 SQ. = 2 IN

Gilia

California poppy

Hepetica

Clover

Black-eyed Susan

Queen Anne's Lace

and stapled to the back of the plywood. Apply a layer of glue to one side of the plywood frame and stretch the canvas in place on top of the glue. Staple the edges in back and let dry.

Cut half-round molding to fit the inside and outside edges of the frame, mitering the corners. Paint the molding green and glue the pieces in place on the frame. Attach mirror to back of frame with brackets.

Work wildflowers in colors indicated on patterns, *except* on the mirror frame eliminate flower C of the Black-eyed Susan design and work petals of violets in varying shades of purple with centers in yellow and gold.

Pillows

A Primer of Design and Pattern

Pillows are pretty, practical, and small enough to be a perfect showcase for needlepoint stitches and patterns. Begin with a pillow to master a new stitch or technique, then try a larger project. Among our pillows, you'll find a wealth of designs to perk up your stitchery repertoire, starting with the "woven" pillows shown here, in which the design is made by the stitches themselves (directions are on the next page). Following those are easy-to-stitch variegated-yarn pillows and some old favorites—patterns from quilts and a farmer's kerchief—as well as an elegant floral design and a sampler pillow. See page 28 for directions for assembling your pillow.

"Woven" Pillows *(shown on pages 24 and 25)*

The outstanding texture and pattern of some needlepoint stitches show to best advantage when the stitches are worked in simple box-and-border designs, as the pillows shown on pages 24 and 25 illustrate. Needlepoint these pillows in weaving, long-arm cross-, wheat-sheaf, and Scotch stitches.

Materials

For each pillow:
18x18 inches #5-count rug canvas
#13 tapestry needle
½ yard off-white brushed corduroy (backing)
Polyester fiberfill

White and Rust Pillow

70-yard skeins (2 ounces each) 3-ply Bucilla Multi-Craft Yarn, or a similar substitute, in the following amounts and colors: 2 off-white and 1 rust
1⅔ yards ⅞-inch-wide off-white grosgrain ribbon

White and Blue Pillow

Two 70-yard skeins (2 ounces each) 3-ply off-white Bucilla Multi-Craft Yarn
3½ yards blue 3-ply yarn
1¼ yards ⅝-inch-wide blue grosgrain ribbon
1⅔ yards ⅞-inch-wide blue grosgrain ribbon

White, Blue, and Green Pillow

70-yard skeins (2 ounces each) 3-ply Bucilla Multi-Craft Yarn, or a suitable substitute, in the following amounts and colors: 2 off-white, 1 blue, and 1 green

Directions

Bind the edges of the canvas with masking tape. Then mark the center horizontal and vertical threads and mount the canvas in a frame for working, if desired.

Following charts opposite, work pillows in stitches indicated. Note that each chart is for one portion of a pillow; reverse as necessary to complete the design. The weaving stitch, long-arm cross-stitch, and wheat-sheaf stitch are explained below. For an explanation of the remaining stitches, see pages 93 to 96. Complete each pillow front as indicated in the directions below, then assemble the pillows following directions on page 28.

White and Rust Pillow

To begin, count down six rows and over six rows from the center of the canvas. Begin stitching in the lower left corner of the center square, following the diagram opposite. In row 1, work a half cross-stitch in every other mesh across the canvas. For row 2, work back across the row from right to left, making a reversed continental stitch over two rows of canvas, with the lower edge of the stitch in the same mesh as the lower edge of the half cross-stitches (see pattern diagram). For row 3, start in the mesh that the second row passed over; work half cross-stitches over two rows of canvas. For row 4, start in the mesh that row 3 passed over; work reversed continental stitches over two rows of canvas. Continue until the last row, then repeat row 1. Finish with one fill-in stitch at the end of each line of the pattern.

To work the border of rust long-arm cross-stitches, begin at the left end of the row. First work a single cross-stitch over two threads of the canvas. Then bring the needle up again at the beginning of the cross-stitch, carry it across four threads and up two, and reinsert in the canvas as shown in the diagram opposite. Bring it straight down two threads and up again. Then carry it back four threads and across two; reinsert in the canvas at the first cross-stitch, making an elongated cross. Bring the needle across two threads (on the underside) and down two threads (on the underside) and to the front again. Repeat the steps above, making the next stitch. At the end of the row, work a cross-stitch over two rows as a filler stitch, turn the canvas, and continue.

Work the remainder of the pillow front in weaving and long-arm cross-stitches, as indicated on the pattern. Finish by working one row of white continental stitches around the last rust border.

Block the completed pillow, following directions on page 9. Then stitch grosgrain ribbon to the edge of the pillow front, between the last row of the border and the row of continental stitches.

White and Blue Pillow

Machine-stitch grosgrain ribbon to canvas between threads 21 and 24 (counted from the center), carefully mitering corners. Just inside the ribbon on the left side, work a row of wheat-sheaf stitches as shown opposite. For each stitch, work five upright Gobelin stitches over four rows of canvas. Then bring the needle up under the center (third) stitch but slide it under the two right-hand stitches and bring it out on the right side of the upright stitches. Carry yarn to the left, across the five stitches. Tuck the needle under the stitches and reinsert it in the canvas under the center (third) stitch, pulling snugly so upright stitches fan out. Each set of stitches shares a mesh with the

White and blue pillow

Grosgrain Ribbon

1 Square = 1 Stitch

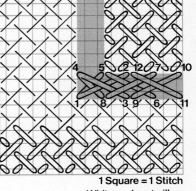

4 5 2 12 7 10
1 8 3 9 6 11

1 Square = 1 Stitch
White and rust pillow

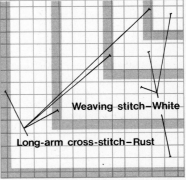

Weaving stitch—White
Long-arm cross-stitch—Rust

1 Square = 1 Inch
White and rust pillow

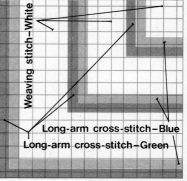

Weaving stitch—White
Long-arm cross-stitch—Blue
Long-arm cross-stitch—Green

1 Square = 1 Inch
White, blue, and green pillow

adjoining set, as shown in the diagram. To finish, work an upright cross-stitch over two rows of canvas between each set of sheaf stitches. Then work a row of backstitches between the ribbon and the sheaf stitches to cover canvas threads.

Next, fill the center with weaving stitches. Work outer border in Scotch stitches, forming a checkerboard design as shown in the pattern diagram. After completing Scotch stitches, work a blue upright cross-stitch in the middle of each set of four squares and wrap yarn around the cross, forming a mock French knot.

Finish the outer border by working upright stitches as indicated on the pattern and covering them with cross-stitches as shown. Work one row of white continental stitches around the design. Block the completed pillow front, following directions on page 9. Then stitch blue grosgrain ribbon to the outer edge of the pillow, following directions for the rust and white pillow. Assemble following directions on page 28.

White, Blue, and Green Pillow
Work in weaving stitches and long-arm cross-stitches, following directions for the rust and white pillow. After the needlepoint is completed, block the pillow, following directions on page 9. Assemble the pillow, following directions on page 28.

Designs with Variegated Yarn

Variegated knitting yarn can add a new twist to traditional needlepoint! The changing colors form brilliant patterns in the two simple-to-stitch pillows, opposite.

The pillow on the left is worked entirely in basket-weave stitches for diagonal rows of color. The one in the chair is a combination of diagonal basket-weave stitches and horizontal continental stitches worked in boxes.

Materials

(For each pillow)
16x20 inches #10-count canvas
Two 3½-ounce skeins 4-ply
   Coats and Clark Mexicana
   variegated knitting yarn, or a
   similar substitute
#18 tapestry needle
Masking tape
Waterproof marking pen
½ yard navy or yellow backing
   fabric
Polyester fiberfill

Directions
Plain Variegated Pillow

Using a waterproof marking pen, draw a 12x16-inch rectangle on the canvas, leaving a two-inch border around each side. Bind the edges of the canvas with masking tape to prevent raveling, and mount the canvas in a frame, if desired.

Begin working the design in either the lower left or upper right corner. Work the entire pillow in basket-weave stitches, referring to the Glossary on pages 93 to 96 for stitch how-to, if necessary.

The changing colors in the variegated yarn create the pattern. To vary the pattern, work small sections rather than entire rows. For example, stitch several inches of basket-weave stitches at a time. If the colors begin to run together and change too often so that the design begins to look busy, work the pillow in smaller sections, referring to the photograph for ideas. But work an entire row every so often to make colors look brighter and more distinct.

Vary the positions in which rows begin and end, making some rows longer than others.

Block the pillow, following the directions on page 9. Trim the canvas margins to within one inch of the needlepoint. Cut backing fabric to match the pillow front, and assemble the pillow following the directions below.

Variegated Pillow with Squares

Using a waterproof pen, draw an 11x14½-inch rectangle (centered) on the canvas. Bind the edges of the canvas with masking tape and mount the canvas in a frame for working, if desired.

Following the pattern below at left, mark twelve 2½-inch squares (25x25 threads) with a waterproof pen. Leave six threads between each square and twelve threads around the outside edges, as shown in the pattern.

Work the squares in horizontal rows using continental stitches. Then fill the background with basket-weave stitches worked on the diagonal. Because of the variegated yarn and the two different stitches, the squares will contrast with the background.

Block the pillow, following directions on page 9; trim the canvas to within one inch of the needlepoint. Cut backing fabric to match canvas, and assemble the pillow following directions below.

How to Assemble a Pillow

To assemble your pillow, cut backing fabric the same size as the pillow front. If desired, add welting as follows. Cut cable cord to go in seam of pillow front, plus two inches. Cut and piece 1½-inch-wide bias strips of fabric to cover cording. Using a zipper foot, machine-stitch fabric over cording. Baste cording to pillow front between the first and second rows of needlepoint.

With right sides facing, stitch pillow front to back on three sides, between first and second rows of needlepoint. Leave one side open for turning. Clip corners and trim the seam margin to ½ inch. Turn right side out, stuff, and slip-stitch the opening.

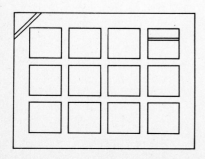

Quilt-Pattern Pillow—Attic Windows Design

Patterns from quilts make beautiful and charming motifs for creative stitchery. This attic windows design, for example, is a traditional pattern popular among our pioneer ancestors. To duplicate it, work a mini-quilt in needlepoint using tapestry wool on #14-count canvas, and finish it as a pillow.

Materials
42 yards light blue tapestry yarn
16 yards dark rust tapestry yarn
32 yards tapestry yarn in each of the following colors: navy blue, light rust, medium rust, white, gold, and dark blue
58 yards gray tapestry yarn for border around pillow
17x17-inch piece #14-count canvas
#18 tapestry needle
Masking tape
Waterproof marking pen
½ yard gray backing fabric
Polyester fiberfill

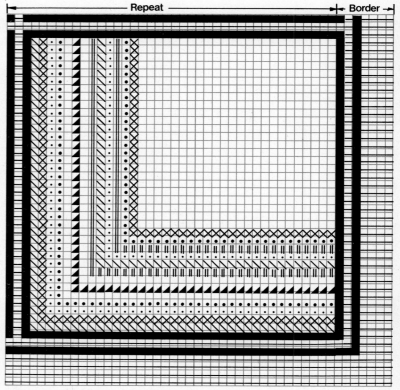

■ Navy	◢ Dark Rust	⟍ Light Rust	□ Light Blue
• Gold	× Medium Rust	‖ Dark Blue	— Gray
			· White

1 Square = 1 Stitch

Directions
The pattern above is for the square in the lower right corner of the pillow and the border design. Repeat it 16 times, in four rows of four squares each, to make the pillow 12½ inches square.

Using a waterproof pen, draw a 12½x12½-inch square in the center of the canvas. Bind the edges of the canvas with masking tape to prevent raveling, and if desired, mount the canvas in a frame to prevent distortion and minimize the need for blocking.

Use complete strands of tapestry yarn for stitching, and begin and end each strand with a waste knot to reduce bulk on the back of the canvas. Beginning in the lower right corner of the canvas, stitch the border design and square, following the color key. Work single rows of color in continental stitches, but work the upper right square in each block with basket-weave stitches, referring to the Glossary on pages 93 to 96 for stitch explanations, if necessary. Then stitch the remainder of the pillow as indicated above, following the "repeat" and "border" notations on the pattern.

Block the finished canvas, following the directions on page 9. Trim unworked canvas to within ½ inch of the needlepoint; cut backing fabric to match. Assemble the pillow following the directions on page 28.

Quilt-Pattern Pillow— Chrysanthemum Bargello Design

The "chrysanthemum" was a popular quilt motif a hundred years ago, and today it's still as appealing. To enjoy it even more, why not needlepoint this charming design?

Each "block" of the needlepoint mini-quilt, opposite, is worked in bargello and tent stitches, with a diamond-eye stitch in the center. Stitch nine flower motifs, then work the background in basket-weave stitches until the pillow is 15 inches square.

Materials

19x19 inches #12-count canvas
#18 tapestry needle
3-ply Persian yarn in the following colors: olive green, dark yellow, medium yellow, and brick red
½ yard green velveteen
1¾ yards cable cord (optional)
Graph paper (10 squares per inch)
Needlepoint frame (optional)

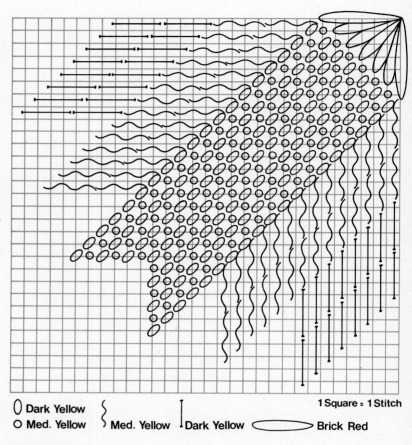

1 Square = 1 Stitch

◊ Dark Yellow
○ Med. Yellow
⟩ Med. Yellow
⎸ Dark Yellow
⬭ Brick Red

Directions

The pattern above is for one-fourth of one of the motifs in the pillow. Transfer it to graph paper, reversing as necessary to complete it. The center stitch, horizontally and vertically, is worked only once. The design is worked nine times on the pillow, in three rows of three motifs each, and the points on each star share a mesh with the points of the adjoining stars. You may transfer the entire pillow design to graph paper, or work from the chart.

Bind the edges of the canvas with masking tape, and mount the canvas in a frame, if desired. Begin stitching in one corner, leaving a 2-inch margin of unworked canvas. Using full, 3-ply strands of wool, stitch the arms of the motif in bargello and tent stitches, as indicated on the pattern. Work the center in a diamond-eye stitch. Finally, work the background in green basket-weave stitches, adding four additional rows around the edges of the motifs. For an explanation of the stitches, see the Glossary on pages 93 to 96.

Block the finished needlepoint following the directions on page 9. Then cut backing fabric to size and use remaining fabric to cover cording, if desired. Assemble the pillow following the directions on page 28.

Bandana Design

Delightful pillow patterns sometimes come from unlikely places! The design opposite, for example, was inspired by a traditional red kerchief. While basket-weave stitches are used for the background, Smyrna stitches and cross-stitches also add textural interest to this old-fashioned and familiar design.

Materials

16x16 inches #10-count canvas
3-ply Paternayan Persian wool
   yarn, or a similar substitute,
   in the following amounts and
   colors: 95 yards #R69 red,
   20 yards #105 dark brown,
   and 20 yards #005 white
#18 tapestry needle
Masking tape
Graph paper
Needlepoint frame (optional)
½ yard dark brown velveteen
   for backing
1½ yards cable cord
Polyester fiberfill

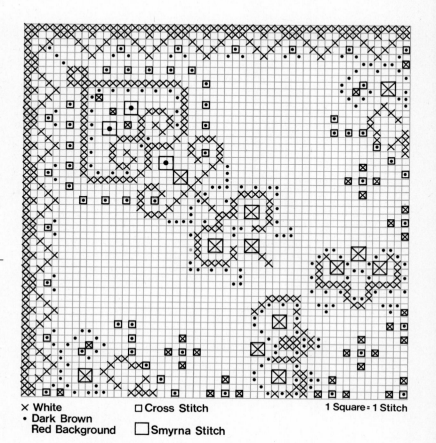

× White
• Dark Brown
   Red Background

☐ Cross Stitch

☐ Smyrna Stitch

1 Square = 1 Stitch

Directions

The pattern above represents one quarter of this 12x12-inch pillow design. Transfer it to graph paper and complete the design by flopping the pattern three times to produce the entire pillow.

Bind the edges of the canvas with masking tape to prevent raveling, and label the top so you are careful not to turn or twist the canvas as you work. Mount the canvas in a frame to minimize distortion, if desired.

Begin working the design from the pattern, using full 3-ply strands of yarn and leaving a 2-inch margin for blocking around the edges. Work the brown and white designs in continental, Smyrna, and cross-stitches before filling in the red background in basket-weave stitches. Refer to the Glossary on pages 93 to 96 for an explanation of the stitches, if necessary.

When the pattern is complete, add five rows of red basket-weave stitches around the outside edges so none of the design is lost when the pillow is assembled.

Block the canvas, following the directions on page 9. Then trim the margin of the canvas, cover the cable cord, cut the velveteen backing, and assemble the pillow following directions on page 28.

Wedding Ring Pillow

Special occasions call for special tributes, such as the lovely wedding ring pillow, opposite. To stitch up this romantic design, use cashmere and cross-stitches in the border, and basket-weave and continental stitches for the blocks of flowers. Between each block, work a stylized wedding ring in mosaic stitches. The finished pillow is 12 inches square.

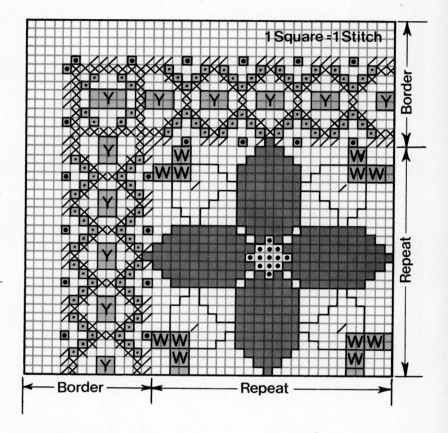

1 Square = 1 Stitch

Border

Repeat

Border — Repeat

Materials

16x16 inches #14-count canvas
1 ounce (approximately 44 yards) #743 blue 3-ply Paternayan Persian wool yarn, or a similar substitute
½ ounce (approximately 22 yards) #590 green 3-ply Paternayan Persian wool yarn, or a similar substitute
40-yard skeins Elsa Williams wool tapestry yarn, or a similar substitute, in the following amounts and colors: 2 #N105 pink, 2 #N304 yellow, 2 #N805 off-white, 1 #N900 white, and 1 #N401 dark green
#19 tapestry needle
Masking tape
Graph paper
½ yard pale green velveteen
Polyester fiberfill
1½ yards cable cord

Color Key

- ⊙ Dark Green Continental Stitch
- ● Dark Green Cross-Stitch
- W White Mosaic Stitch
- ⊡ Blue Cross-Stitch
- Y Yellow Cashmere Stitch
- ☐ White Continental Stitch
- ⊠ Pink
- ⬚ Green

Directions

The pattern above represents the upper left corner of the pillow. Transfer it to graph paper and continue charting the design until there are 25 flower motifs (five rows of five flowers each), following the repeats indicated on the pattern.

Bind the edges of the canvas with masking tape and mount the canvas in a frame, if desired. Begin working the design, leaving a 2-inch margin of unworked canvas around the edges. Use 2-ply strands of Persian wool yarn and full strands of tapestry yarn.

Work the pink, yellow, and blue flowers in basket-weave stitches; then work the pale green leaves and the dark green centers in continental stitches. Fill in the background in basket-weave stitches, and work the white squares in mosaic stitches. Work the border design one color at a time in the stitches indicated on the chart. For stitch how-to and diagrams, see the Glossary on pages 93 to 96.

Block the finished canvas following the directions on page 9. Trim the unworked canvas to within ½ inch of the needlepoint.

Cut green velveteen the same size as the needlepoint-canvas. Then use remaining velveteen to cut and piece 1¼-inch bias strips to cover cording. Assemble the pillow following the directions on page 28.

Paper-Doll Sampler Pillow

A variety of pleasing needlepoint patterns that combine different stitches and techniques are used in this sampler pillow. Although the dolls are worked in basket-weave stitches, the cream-colored background is worked in reverse basket-weave — a technique that leaves the "weaving" pattern on the finished side. The border is divided into sections so you can practice a number of stitches, working each design as explained at right.

Materials

16x16 inches #10-count canvas
3-ply strands of Persian wool
 yarn in cream, red, pink,
 light yellow, medium yellow,
 light turquoise, medium
 turquoise, medium green,
 dark green, medium orange,
 dark orange, light brown,
 and medium brown
#18 tapestry needle
Waterproof marking pen
Masking tape
1½ yards calico fabric
Polyester fiberfill

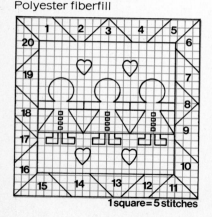

1 square = 5 stitches

Directions

Tape the edges of the canvas and, using a waterproof pen, draw a 90x90-mesh square in the center. Then mark a border 16 meshes wide around the square. Enlarge the pattern and transfer it to canvas, following the directions on page 42. (Dolls are 30 stitches wide.)

Using full 3-ply strands of yarn, work light-colored background stitches first so darker colors do not show through. Refer to the Glossary on pages 93 to 96 for an explanation of stitches.

Work dolls and hearts in basket-weave stitches and buttons in Smyrna stitches, referring to the photograph for colors. Use reverse basket-weave stitches for the background. Work a row of brown continental stitches around the square and to divide the border into sections. Work each section following the specific directions below.

1 — Vertical orange stripes: Work dark orange rows in Smyrna stitches with two rows of continental stitches between (one in light orange and one in cream).

2 — Diagonal turquoise stripes: Work in continental stitches, making each diagonal line two stitches wide. Use any combination of light turquoise, dark turquoise, and cream.

3 — Yellow and cream checks: Work the cream-colored cross-stitches first, with one row of yellow continental stitches between.

4 and 14 — Gingham checks: Work in Scotch stitches, using the medium color in every row; then alternate dark and light colors.

5, 12, and 20 — Polka dots: Alternate a solid row of tent stitches with one leaving every fourth stitch blank. Fill with red, turquoise, or brown.

6 — Green and turquoise vertical stripes: Work the medium and dark turquoise rows in cashmere stitches with two rows of continental stitches (one in cream and one in green) between.

7 — Yellow checks: Work in yellow and cream mosaic stitches.

8 — Brown checkerboard: Work the vertical rows in upright Gobelin and continental stitches. Work the horizontal rows in slanting Gobelin and continental stitches. Fill with cream continental stitches.

9 — Tulips: Work flowers in pink and red tent stitches.

10 — Orange squares: Work cream-colored Scotch-stitch squares in opposite directions, with orange continental stitches between.

11 — Horizontal stripes: Work green and cream continental stitches.

13 — Yellow vertical stripes: Work cream rows in mosaic stitches, with light yellow Smyrna stitches between.

15 — Brown horizontal stripes: Dark brown stripes are slanting Gobelin stitches; work brown and cream cross-stitch tramé between.

16 — Oranges: Work in shades of orange and green as shown.

17 — Vertical turquoise stripes: Work two rows of tent stitches in light turquoise with cream-colored cross-stitches between.

18 — Green hearts: Work as shown in the photograph.

19 — Red and pink horizontal stripes: Work cream-colored stripes in upright Gobelin stitches. Work red and pink rows of continental stitches between. Alternate directions of stitches.

To finish the pillow, block the canvas following the directions on page 9. Cut a 4-inch-wide strip of calico fabric and fold it in half across the width. Baste the two long ends together and gently pull the stitches to gather the fabric. Baste the ruffle around the pillow so the ruffle lies against the right side of the canvas.

Trim the canvas margins to ½ inch and cut a piece of calico fabric to match. Assemble the pillow following the directions on page 28.

Adventures in Needlepoint

Unique Projects to Stitch

Needlepoint can be fresh and imaginative! To prove it, here's a section filled with adventurous stitchery. For example, why not work in the round —to create a scenic hassock —or make delightful bride and groom dolls? Or adapt motifs, such as our children's artwork, shown below. Directions are on the next page.

Adapting Designs for Needlepoint

Once you've learned your needlepoint stitches, you may wish to try your hand at designing your own piece of needlepoint. Then you'll be sure the finished product fits your needs exactly and you'll have the satisfaction of being your own designer.

Here are some pointers to get you started, as well as basic how-to for enlarging, reducing, and transferring designs – either your own or those in this book.

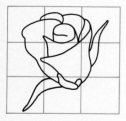

The original pattern

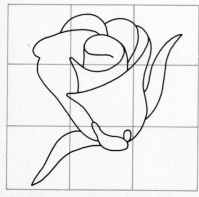

Enlarging on a grid

Before You Begin

First, decide what to stitch. Will it be a chair seat, a picture, a pillow? How large will it be? And where will it go? The room in which a stitchery will live can greatly influence its design.

On a piece of paper, draw an accurate outline, like an empty picture frame, around your proposed project. Do your drawing and sketching on tracing paper placed over this outline "frame" to be sure the finished design will be the right size and shape.

Designing Methods

There are as many ways to begin designing as there are needlework designers. Here are some of the more widely used techniques.

Try tracing shapes from existing designs and rearranging them within the outline frame. Pictures from magazines, books, greeting cards, and coloring books and motifs from printed textiles such as slipcovers are good sources. A photograph, a child's artwork, or a rubbing from a furniture carving can also be your starting point.

Choose a pattern appropriate to the area where it will be placed. If you use a motif from a room's carved woodwork to inspire a pillow border, the pillow will belong in that room. Look around the work's future home for designs. Then photograph, trace, rub, or sketch them.

Borrowing designs from nature is also exciting and challenging. Cut a melon or tomato in half and study its patterns. Look at shells, areas of tree bark, or wave lines on a beach. Sketch or photograph what you see. A camera reduces three-dimensional nature to two dimensions, making the designer's job easier. Eliminate nonessential details and you may have an exciting, totally original design.

For a more contemporary or even abstract design, work with paper shapes, following the directions on page 70.

Enlarging and Reducing Designs

Once you have a design, it may be the wrong size for your project. There are several ways to enlarge or reduce it.

Working With a Photostat

The easiest way to change the size of the design is to take it to a blueprint company. Ask for a "positive copy" of the design, specifying the dimensions you want. When the copy is ready, draw black outlines around the important shapes; omit unimportant details. Then draw your outline frame around the design and the pattern is complete.

Enlarging With a Grid

Some designs, such as many in this book, are marked with a grid — small squares laid over the design. With others, such as original designs of your own, you may wish to add a grid. To do so, tape the pattern to a table and secure a sheet of clear plastic over it. Using a fine-tip marking pen, rule the plastic into ½-inch squares, making a grid such as the one at left.

Next, enlarge or reduce the design by drawing a second grid on tissue or brown paper, following the scale indicated on the pattern, if there is one. If there is no scale, mark your outline frame with the same number of squares as are on the plastic sheet.

Next, number the horizontal and vertical rows of squares in the margin of the original pattern. Transfer these numbers to the corresponding rows on the new pattern.

Begin by finding a square on your grid that corresponds with a square on the original. Mark your grid wherever a design line intersects a line on the original. (Visually divide every line into fourths to gauge whether the design line cuts the grid line halfway or somewhere in between.)

Working one square at a time, mark each grid line where it is intersected by the design. After marking several squares, connect the dots, following the contours of the original as shown in the lower diagrams, opposite. Work in pencil so you can erase.

Patterns Without Grids
To enlarge or reduce a design without a grid, you need to know at least one of the dimensions of the final pattern. Draw a box around the original design. Then draw a diagonal line between two opposite corners.

On the pattern paper, draw a right angle and extend the bottom line to the length of the new pattern. Lay the original in the corner and, using a ruler, extend the diagonal. Then draw a perpendicular line between the diagonal and the end of the bottom line, as shown at right.

Divide the original and the new pattern into quarters, number the sections, and transfer the design as explained above (see diagrams at right).

Transferring Designs
To transfer your design to canvas, use waterproof marking pens, following the directions on page 10. Or, paint the canvas with artist's acrylic paints, following directions below.

Painting a Canvas
To paint a needlepoint canvas, you'll need some tools and equipment. Gather together artist's acrylic paints in the appropriate colors; a palette or palette paper; palette knife; small-,

medium-, and large-pointed brushes; and a spray bottle of water. Acrylic paints are nice to use because they dry quickly, mix and clean up with water, and are waterproof when dry. They also come in a wide range of colors and are easy to mix.

Begin by taping your design to a flat surface. Cover it with a sheet of clear plastic if you wish to save it. Center the canvas over the picture, allowing at least two inches of canvas to extend beyond the design frame on all sides. (You'll need this margin around the needlepoint for blocking and finishing later.) Tape the canvas in place.

If you discover that your design is hard to see beneath the canvas, trace the predominant lines on the pattern with a fine-tip black marking pen.

Put a small daub of each of the colors you intend to use on your palette. When you're ready to use a color, spray a little water on it and mix the paint with the palette knife until it is smooth and the consistency of whipped cream. The paint should flow evenly onto the canvas, but not drip through it.

Use the small brush for fine details and outlining, the medium brush for slightly larger areas, and the large brush for the background. Start by outlining the main parts of the design. When this paint dries, add color in adjacent areas. Wash brushes in water before changing colors.

If paint covers the spaces in the canvas, use a toothpick to clear them. Allow the painted canvas to dry thoroughly.

To test the quality of the paint, sprinkle water over a sample of painted canvas. If the color runs slightly, spray the painted canvas *very lightly* with clear acrylic to keep colors from running and spoiling the stitchery when the piece is blocked.

Enlarging without a grid

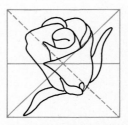

Segmenting the original

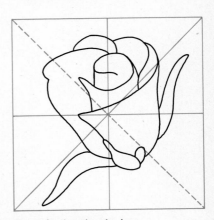

Transferring the design

Chinese Dollhouse Rug

Designed to resemble an antique Oriental rug, this elegant miniature is stitched small-scale on #18-count canvas. The tiny continental and basket-weave stitches give the design fine detail and make it perfect for dollhouses or miniature room displays.

Materials
11x14 inches #18-count canvas
3-ply Paternayan Persian yarn,
    or a similar substitute, in the
    following amounts and
    colors: 14 yards #266 dark
    rust, 22 yards #274 medium
    rust, 6 yards #287 light rust,
    22 yards #005 white, 5 yards
    #314 dark blue, 10 yards
    #380 medium blue,
    8 yards #381
    medium-light blue,
    and 5 yards #382
    light blue
40 yards fine linen
    macrame cord
    (fringe)
Waterproof marking
    pen
Masking tape
11x13 inches rust
    velveteen
#22 tapestry needle
Colored pencils
    (optional)
Graph paper
    (optional)
Needlepoint frame
    (optional)

Color Key
■ **dark rust**
▨ **med. ”**
□ **light ”**
□ **white**
▨ **dark blue**
▨ **med. ”**
▨ **med. lt. ”**
□ **light ”**

Directions
The pattern below represents one quadrant of the finished rug. You may stitch from the chart, or transfer it to graph paper with colored pencils, reversing as necessary to complete the design.

Mark the center of the canvas with a waterproof pen, and bind the edges with masking tape to prevent raveling. If desired, mount the canvas in a needlepoint frame to minimize distortion.

Use one strand of yarn throughout, and begin stitching in the center of the design if you are working from the chart. Stitch small details in continental stitches and larger areas in basket-weave stitches (stitch directions are on pages 93 to 96).

Block the finished rug following the directions on page 9, and trim the unworked canvas to within ½ inch of the needlepoint. Cut a piece of backing fabric to match. With the right sides facing, sew pieces together, leaving one end open. Turn, press, and slip-stitch.

For the fringe, cut two 27-inch pieces of cord and approximately 155 pieces each 2½ inches long. Thread a long piece into a needle and tie it into a lark's head knot in the corner mesh in the last row of needlepoint at one end of the rug. Adjust the ends of the yarn so one end is about 1½ inches long. The longer, outside end will be the bearer cord for the knots that make the fringe. Tie remaining short cords into alternate spaces in the canvas along the last row of stitching, making sure ends are even. Tie all short cords into two rows of knots, as illustrated on page 46. Repeat for the other end of the rug. To finish, trim ends evenly.

Indian Dollhouse Rug

An authentic Navajo Indian design makes a striking 7½ x 10½-inch rug when stitched on #18-count canvas. To fringe the ends, tie fine linen cord in double half-hitch knots as explained below.

Materials

10x13 inches #18-count canvas
#22 tapestry needle
3-ply Paternayan Persian yarn, or a suitable substitute, in the following amounts and colors: 22 yards #050 black, 22 yards #411 brown, 8 yards #005 white, 4 yards #162 dark gray, and 12 yards #166 light gray
40 yards fine linen macrame cord
Waterproof marking pen
9x12 inches black velveteen
Masking tape

Horizontal double half-hitch knot

Directions

The pattern, opposite, represents one quadrant of the finished rug. You may stitch from the chart, or transfer it to graph paper with colored pencils, reversing as necessary to complete the design.

Mark the center of the canvas with a waterproof pen and bind the edges with masking tape to prevent raveling. If desired, mount the canvas in a needlepoint frame to minimize distortion.

Use one strand of yarn throughout, and begin stitching in the center of the design if you are working from the chart. If you've made a colored graph of the pattern, begin stitching in the upper right corner, but leave approximately 1½ inches of unworked canvas around the design. Stitch small details in continental stitches and larger areas in basket-weave stitches. For an explanation of each of these stitches, see pages 93 to 96.

Block the finished rug, following the directions on page 9. Then trim the unworked canvas to within ½ inch of the needlepoint and cut backing fabric to match. With right sides facing, sew the backing to the needlepoint, leaving one end open. Turn, press lightly, and slip-stitch the opening.

For the fringe, cut two 24-inch pieces of fine linen cord and approximately 130 pieces each 2½ inches long. Thread one of the long pieces into a needle and tie it into a lark's head knot in the corner mesh in the last row of needlepoint at one end of the rug. Adjust the yarn so one end is about 1½ inches long. The longer, outside end will be the bearer cord for the knots that make the fringe. Tie short cords into alternate spaces in the canvas along the last row of stitching, making sure ends are even. Tie short cords into two rows of double half-hitch knots (see below).

How to Make a Fringe with Double Half-Hitch Knots

To make this decorative fringe, first tie on the cords for the knots, as indicated in the directions above and on page 44. The outside cord, number 1 in the diagram at left, should be the longer of the two cords tied in the first knot. It is the bearer cord around which all of the double half-hitch knots are tied.

Stabilize the rug and bearer cord by thumbtacking them to a cork or macrame board. Tack the bearer cord on the left to hold it in place. Then carry it across the rug and tack it off to the side so it is straight and taut at all times.

For each knot, wrap the end of a short cord around the bearer cord twice, as shown in the diagram (see cord 2). Push loops close together. Then wrap the next knot (with cord 3), using your fingers to snug it close to the previous one. The bearer cord should be completely hidden by the knots that are made over it.

At the end of the first row of knots, unpin the bearer cord, bend it back along the first row of knots, and re-tack it in position for the second row of knots. When all knots are tied, trim fringe to ½ inch so ends are even.

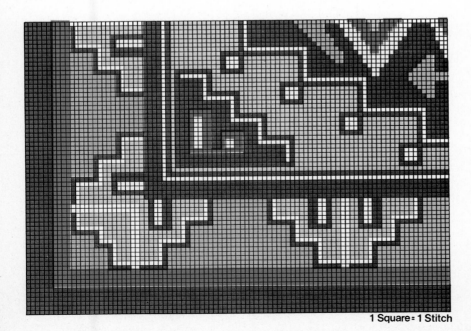

Color Key
- ■ black
- ▨ brown
- □ white
- ▨ dark grey
- ▨ light grey

1 Square = 1 Stitch

Needlepoint Flowers

Needlepoint petals keep these flowers beautiful year after year. Worked in basket-weave stitches, each petal is gracefully shaped with copper wire.

Materials

(For three 5-petal flowers — one large and two small)

1 yard #10-count penelope canvas

1 skein 3-ply Persian yarn in each of the following colors: dark, medium, and light pink and magenta (or four shades of purple), and white,

¾ yard medium-weight fabric (for backing)

Small pearl or silver beads

1 spool copper bead wire

1 package green plastic tape or florist's tape

6½ yards medium-gauge copper wire

#17 tapestry needle

Waterproof marking pen

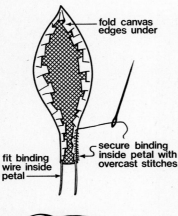

fold canvas edges under

secure binding inside petal with overcast stitches

fit binding wire inside petal

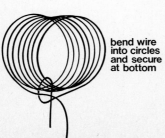

bend wire into circles and secure at bottom

Directions

Note: Flowers are about six and ten inches across.

Cut ten 4x7-inch pieces of canvas for the small petals and five 5x8-inch pieces for the large petals. Using a waterproof pen, transfer the petal designs at right to the canvas.

Work each petal in basket-weave stitches, following the color key and substituting shades of lavender for the pink, if desired. Use full strands of yarn throughout. Work outer edges of each petal first. Then fill the center vein with magenta or dark purple and stitch remainder of petal.

After finishing a petal, cut around the needlepoint, leaving ½ inch of unworked canvas. Carefully fold under the canvas edges and steam-press.

Cut copper wire 14 inches long for small petals and 17 inches long for large petals. Bend the wire to fit the outer edge of each petal and slip it beneath the folded edges. Using yarn to match edge of petal, anchor wire in place with closely spaced overcast stitches, as shown at left.

Lay petal on the bias of the backing fabric and cut out backing, adding a ¼-inch seam allowance. Slip-stitch lining to needlepoint, turning in the seam allowance. Complete five petals for each flower.

For centers, cut one yard of bead wire. Tie a knot three inches from one end; string with beads to within four inches of the end. Knot wire again three inches from the end, leaving one inch free between beads and knot.

Loop wire into eight circles; anchor circles together at the bottom with a few twists of the wire ends, as shown at left.

To assemble each flower, grasp five petals in one hand with the ends pointing down. Arrange them so they fan gracefully. Insert free ends of the beaded cluster into the center, and anchor by twisting wires. Wrap additional wire around the bottom of the petals, then cover the wire with florist's tape. Shape the petals by bending the wires in them.

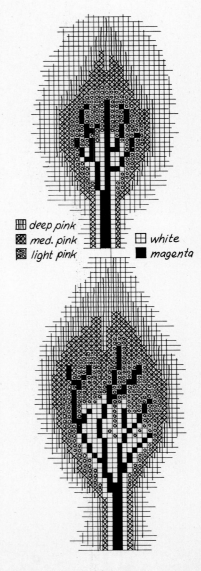

⊞ deep pink
⊠ med. pink
▩ light pink
⊞ white
■ magenta

Mosaic-Pattern Jewel Box

This lovely decorative box is an adventure in easy-to-master needlepoint stitches. The stitches, worked in both wool and cotton yarns, form two different patterns – one for the top of the box and the other for the sides. When the needlepoint is complete, each piece is backed with mat board and then padded and lined with red satin. The patterns at right represent one-fourth of the finished designs.

Materials

3-ply Paternayan yarn, or a
  suitable substitute, in the
  following amounts and
  colors: 45 yards #852 coral,
  12 yards #242 red, and 18
  yards #793 light blue
16-yard twists #3 DMC pearl
  cotton, or a suitable
  substitute, in the following
  amounts and colors: two
  #943 teal blue and one #907
  chartreuse
¼ yard #12-count interlock
  canvas
Two 4½x4½-inch pieces mat
  board
Four 2½x4½-inch pieces mat
  board
#18 tapestry needle
¼ yard red crepe-backed satin
  or lining fabric
Red sewing thread
#7 embroidery needle
Quilt batting
6x6-inch piece red felt
Craft knife
Fabric glue
Clothespins
3 cinnabar beads for trim

Directions

The finished box measures 4¾x4¾x2⅝ inches. Stitch the pieces separately and then sew them together. Cut each piece with about two extra inches of canvas on each side. Bind the canvas edges with masking tape.

Cut four side pieces (7x5 inches) and one top piece (7x7 inches) from canvas and stitch them as shown on the patterns at right. Slant the stitches toward the center. Refer to the Glossary on pages 93 to 96 for an explanation of the stitches.

Stitch one section of color at a time, beginning in the center of each design. Use one strand of pearl cotton and two strands of Persian wool throughout.

When each piece is complete, do one row of continental stitches around all four sides with red yarn. Block the canvas if necessary, following the directions on page 9.

To begin constructing the box, trim the canvas edges to within ½ inch of the stitching.

Glue the mat boards to the backs of the needlepoint pieces, using white glue sparingly. Fold the canvas edges around the boards, using clothespins to hold the edges down. Let dry. Cut and glue a piece of red felt to the sixth piece of mat board.

Cut six pieces of quilt batting to match the six pieces of mat board. Cut two 5½-inch squares and one 3½x20-inch rectangle from the red satin.

Align the four side pieces to make one long row. Match the quilt batting with the mat boards (with the needlepoint side face-down). Then, pin the satin to the batting along the edges, turning the raw edges under. Whipstitch the satin to the needlepoint. String three beads on red yarn and insert the end of the yarn into the top before stitching the satin.

Fold the long piece into four

sides and whipstitch the seams. Attach the bottom piece, felt side down. Attach the top on one side (opposite bead handle) the same way you joined the side seams. Keep the stitching fairly loose so the lid lies flat and does not spring open.

Color Key
A Coral
B Red
C Teal blue
D Chartreuse
E Light blue

Stitch Key
1 Mosaic stitch
2 Double leviathan stitch
3 Continental stitch
4 Slanting Gobelin stitch
5 Half-cross-stitch
6 Smyrna stitch

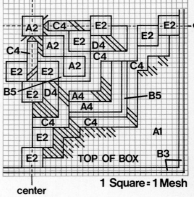

TOP OF BOX
1 Square = 1 Mesh
center

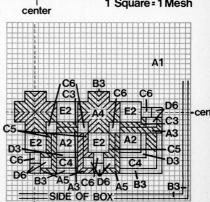

SIDE OF BOX
1 Square = 1 Mesh
center

Bride and Groom Dolls

Adults as well as children will delight in the whimsy and charm of this demure bride and proper bridegroom.

The dolls, which are about 24 inches tall and 10 inches wide, are worked on #14-count canvas in continental and basket-weave stitches. They are good examples of shaped needle-point — pieces that are cut and made three-dimensional rather than left flat for framing or hanging. The patterns are on page 54.

Materials

1 yard #14-count canvas for each doll (see note)
3-ply Paternayan Persian wool yarn, or a similar substitute, in the colors indicated on the pattern on page 54 (see note at right)
#22 tapestry needle
Waterproof marking pen
Masking tape
¾ yard white velveteen (bride)
¾ yard gray velveteen (groom)
Polyester fiberfill

Directions

Note: Both dolls shown opposite were worked on #14-count canvas. They may, however, be worked on larger (or smaller) mesh canvas — or on Penelope canvas, if you wish. The finer the canvas used for the dolls, the more detail you will have in the finished designs.

The amount of yarn you use depends on how tightly you stitch. To judge your own yarn gauge, work one square inch of scrap canvas in basket-weave stitches; measure and note the amount of yarn used as you stitch. Then estimate the total number of square inches in each color in the design and multiply that number by the amount of yarn used to work one square inch. If you are unable to judge the amount of yarn required, enlarge and transfer the pattern to the canvas and work several sample rows. Take the sample with you to your needle-point shop and get help in estimating the amounts of yarn needed. Be sure to buy sufficient yarns in the same dye lots to complete the project so you don't have unattractive variations in the colors.

Following the directions on page 42, enlarge the patterns on page 54 onto a large sheet of paper. Transfer them to canvas as follows: tape the paper pattern to a table or flat surface, then tape canvas over the pattern, leaving at least a 2-inch margin of canvas completely around each pattern for blocking. Using a *light-colored, waterproof pen* (such as pale gray or blue), trace the outlines of the design onto the canvas. If the design is difficult to see under the canvas, trace over outlines with a fine-tip black marking pen. It is not necessary to color the canvas before you begin stitching. For correct placement of colors, simply refer to the numbered sections of the pattern and to the color key on page 54 as you work.

Press the canvas with a dry iron, and bind all the edges with masking tape to keep the canvas from raveling and to prevent yarns from catching in the rough edge of the canvas as you stitch. If desired, mount the canvas in a frame for stitching to minimize distortion as you work.

Using two strands of yarn throughout, outline all areas of the canvas first in a single row of continental stitches in the appropriate colors. Next, work small detail areas. Then work the larger, solid areas of each pattern, such as the bride's gown and veil and the groom's coat, in basket-weave stitches. (Refer to the Glossary on pages 93 to 96 for an explanation of the stitches, if necessary). When each doll is completed, work an additional two rows of continental stitches completely around the outer edges so none of the design is lost when the doll is sewn together. (This extra margin will be taken up in the seam when you sew the needlepoint pieces to the velveteen backing fabrics.)

Block the finished needlepoint, following the directions on page 9.

To assemble the dolls, lay the needlepoint on the velveteen backing, right sides facing. Baste the pieces together to prevent shifting. Machine-stitch around the outlines of each doll, running the machine stitches inside the two extra rows of needlepoint stitches. Stitch again, ⅛ inch outside the first row of stitching. Leave the bottom of the doll open for turning and stuffing. Trim excess canvas and velveteen close to stitching. Carefully turn the doll right side out and press lightly. Stuff both dolls with polyester fiberfill and slip-stitch the bottom edges closed.

continued

Bride and Groom Dolls *(continued)*

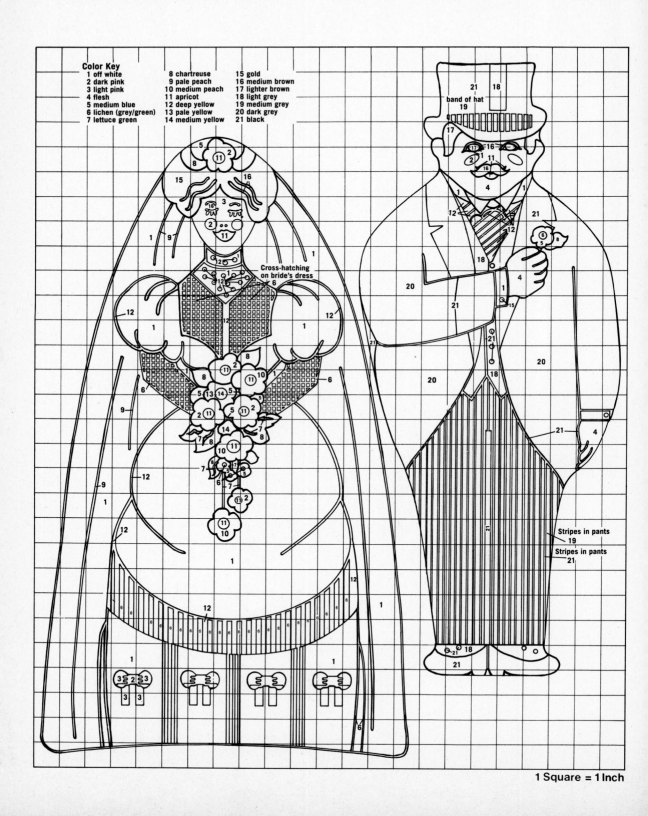

Color Key
1 off white
2 dark pink
3 light pink
4 flesh
5 medium blue
6 lichen (grey/green)
7 lettuce green
8 chartreuse
9 pale peach
10 medium peach
11 apricot
12 deep yellow
13 pale yellow
14 medium yellow
15 gold
16 medium brown
17 lighter brown
18 light grey
19 medium grey
20 dark grey
21 black

band of hat
19

Cross-hatching
on bride's dress

Stripes in pants
19
Stripes in pants
21

1 Square = 1 Inch

Scenic Hassock *(continued on page 56)*

Scenic Hassock *(continued)*

If you're a needlepoint enthusiast who enjoys the challenge of a grand-scale project, you'll love the mural hassock shown on page 55 and closeup, opposite. And it can be stitched in record time, thanks to quickpoint canvas, heavy rug yarn, and a variety of fast-working stitches. For diagrams of the stitches, see pages 93 to 96.

Materials

3⅓ yards #5-count penelope canvas
70-yard skeins Aunt Lydia's rug yarn in the colors and amounts listed in color key
#13 tapestry needle
Masking tape
Graph paper or brown wrapping paper
Shredded foam, polystyrene pellets, or a similar substitute
Waterproof marking pen
Carpet thread
Heavy muslin or lightweight canvas

Directions

Note: The finished hassock is 16 inches high, 26½ inches in diameter, and 86 inches around its circumference.

Enlarge the patterns opposite and below and transfer them to graph paper or brown wrapping paper. Tape the patterns to a flat surface; then tape canvas atop them, leaving a 2-inch margin around the edges of the design. Using a waterproof pen, lightly sketch the outlines of the design onto the canvas.

Using the appropriate color, outline each motif of the landscape with a single row of tent stitches. When one of the larger motifs, such as a hill, is to be stitched in a combination of colors, outline it in the darkest color to be used in that area. All of the smaller motifs are stitched in simple tent stitches; patterned stitches and combinations of colors are used only in larger areas. See the Glossary for pattern diagrams for the stitches.

The lakes, rivers, and meandering path are worked in a combination of colors for a textured effect. For the water, cut two equal lengths of light and dark turquoise, separate each length into three plies, and combine two light plies and one dark ply. Do the same for the path, using two plies of beige and one of dark brown. Outline both the water and path areas with one row of tent stitches in the darker shades.

When stitching the top of the hassock, outline the outer edge in medium blue tent stitches and the clouds in peach tent stitches. Fill clouds with white and cream and the sky with medium blue.

To assemble the hassock, trim the canvas to within one inch of the stitching. Fold the margins under and steam-press. Use carpet thread to whipstitch together the short ends of the long body strip, aligning motifs carefully. Reinforce the seam and cover the whipstitching with yarn to match motifs or sky.

Pin-fit the top to the body of the hassock. Whipstitch top to body and then cover whipstitching with a row of medium blue yarn. Turn the hassock upside down and stuff. For the base, cut a 28½-inch circle of muslin or canvas and pin-fit it to the bottom of the hassock. Whipstitch securely with a double strand of carpet thread.

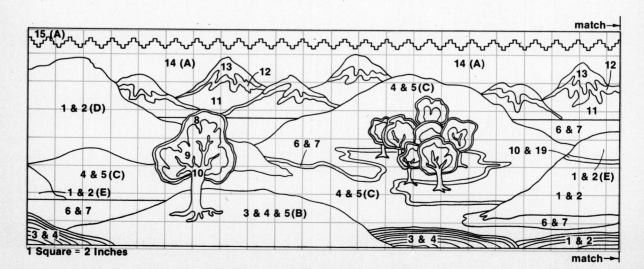

1 Square = 2 Inches

Color Key

1. Burnt orange (3 skeins)
2. Peach (3)
3. Evergreen (3)
4. Grass green (3)
5. Spring green (3)
6. Dark turquoise (2)
7. Light turquoise (2)
8. Emerald (1)
9. Jade (1)
10. Dark brown (1)
11. Purple (2)
12. Lavender (1)
13. Cream (2)
14. Light blue (4)
15. Medium blue (1)
16. White (1)
17. Dark yellow (1)
18. Light yellow (1)
19. Beige (1)

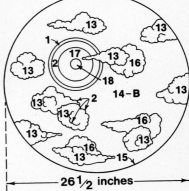

Stitch Guide

A Bargello flat stitch
B Mosaic or Scotch stitch
C Variation on mosaic stitch

D Bargello flat stitch
   variation
E Diagonal flat stitch with
   tent-stitch outline

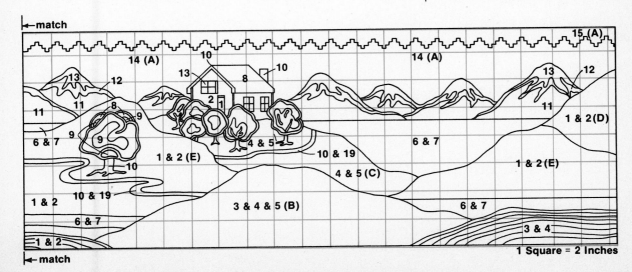

Creative Techniques
New Ways with Needlepoint

Rich with creative possibilities—that's needlepoint! The projects shown here, for example, are stitched with string and the background is left unworked for an airy look (directions are on the next page). To show you some other imaginative uses of the materials and techniques of needlepoint, this section includes bargello patterns worked on a sewing machine or stitched in metallic thread or raffia, a box with inlaid stones, and a free-form stitchery to design yourself.

String Needlepoint — Pillows and Rug (shown on pages 58 and 59)

The light and lacy look of the rug and pillows shown on pages 58 and 59 is actually exposed needlepoint canvas that lets the backing fabric shine through. And, the open canvas further sets off the cotton yarn used for stitching.

So if you think string is just for wrapping around packages and forgetful fingers – think again! It's a stunning material for needlepoint, too.

Materials

20x20 inches #5-count canvas for each pillow
49x76 inches #5-count canvas for rug with 15 squares
Lily "Sugar 'n Cream" cotton yarn (available in 125-yard balls) in the following amounts for each design:
A — 142 yards; B — 136 yards; C — 206 yards; and D — 166 yards
#13 tapestry needle
⅝ yard colored backing fabric for each pillow
Polyester fiberfill
Needlepoint frame or two pairs of 20-inch artist's stretcher strips
Waterproof marking pen
White sewing thread
Staple gun (optional)

Directions

The finished size of each square in the rug and pillows is about 16x16 inches and includes a 12-inch center panel surrounded by a two-inch border. There are four designs in all, shown opposite as A, B, C, and D. The borders for each design are the same.

To make the pillows, bind the edges of the canvas with masking tape. Mount the canvas in a needlepoint frame or staple it to a frame assembled from artist's stretcher strips so you can pull the yarn firmly as you work. The tension applied during stitching creates the lacy, open look of this needlepoint.

Remember that there is a two-inch margin of unworked canvas around all four sides of the design. Each center panel actually measures 61 meshes square, and borders are 10 meshes wide.

Choose one of the four designs to needlepoint, making sure to center the design as it is worked on the canvas. Also allow for the border pattern and the two-inch margin of canvas for blocking and seam allowances or hem.

Cut the yarn into two-yard lengths for easier handling. Thread the needle with one of the lengths and knot the two ends to form a piece of yarn one yard long.

Unlike many needlepoint stitches and patterns, some of these designs are worked easiest from left to right. Follow the stitching sequence indicated by the numbers on each pattern, and draw the threads firmly with each stitch for a pulled-thread effect. Hold the yarn close to the canvas and pull it in the direction of the next stitch to help open the mesh. The doubled yarn will increase the pull on the canvas and produce more of an openwork look than a single thread would. Since you're using doubled lengths of yarn, it is important to keep the strands from twisting so stitches lie flat on the canvas. Every now and then, let the needle fall loosely away from the canvas as you work so the threads will untwist.

Follow the designs opposite, repeating the portion of the pattern shown to complete an entire square. After working the center panel, stitch the border pattern completely around the edge.

When the pillow front is finished, block the needlepoint following the directions on page 9.

To assemble the pillow, cut two pieces of backing fabric to match the size of the canvas. Baste one piece to the back of the canvas. Then, with right sides facing, sew the canvas to the other piece of fabric, leaving one side open for turning. Clip corners and trim the seam allowance to ½ inch. Turn, stuff, and slip-stitch the opening.

To make the rug, use a single piece of canvas; it will measure about 45x72 inches when finished. Draw 15 squares on the canvas using a waterproof pen. Leave a border between each square, and allow a two-inch border of unworked canvas around the edges. Remember that each square is 61 meshes wide and each border is 10 meshes wide. Follow the placement diagram, opposite, for the arrangement of squares and patterns.

Stitch each square, following the directions above. Finish one center panel before starting the next, leaving 10 meshes empty between each panel for the border. Work the border pattern last.

To finish the rug, fold the two-inch margin in half and then turn it to the back of the rug. Stitch it to the back side with double lengths of white sewing thread.

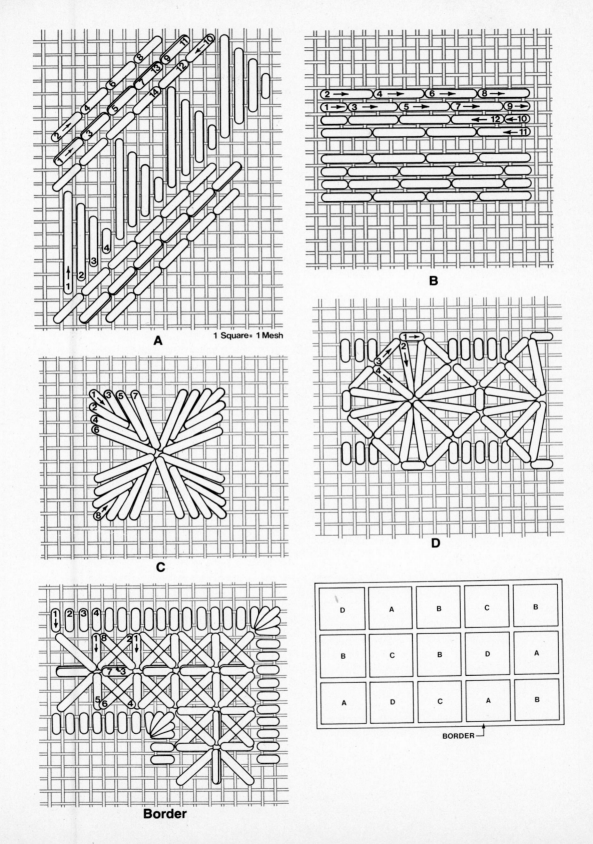

1 Square = 1 Mesh

A

B

C

D

Border

Sewing-Machine Bargello — Chair Seat

Beautiful bargello patterns, like the one shown on this chair seat, can be stitched on a zig-zag sewing machine as well as by hand. And with a little practice, you will see how easy and creative machine-needlepoint can be.

This "domes-and-spires" pattern, done entirely by machine, is worked on #18-count canvas, covering four meshes with each stitch. Stitch each row the same as the first.

Materials

Zig-zag sewing machine
22x22 inches #18-count mono canvas (or size to fit seat)
#20 cotton thread, or any similar substitute, in purple, dark blue, light blue, olive green, yellow, and gold
Sheet of polyester quilt batting
⅜-inch plywood board for seat
White sewing thread for bobbin
Masking tape
Waterproof marking pen
Staple gun or tacks
Soil-retardant spray

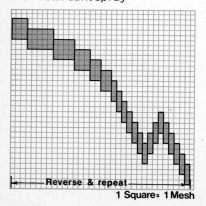

Reverse & repeat
1 Square= 1 Mesh

Directions

Bind the edges of the canvas with masking tape to prevent raveling. Mark the outlines of the chair seat on the canvas with a waterproof marking pen. When stitching the chair seat, extend the pattern at least ½ inch beyond these lines to allow some overlap when the edges are turned under.

Thread the sewing machine with purple thread on top and white in the bobbin. Set the machine for its widest zig-zag stitch, remove the presser foot, and lower the machine's feed dogs. Using a sample piece of canvas, choose a starting point close to one edge. Place your right hand on the wheel of the machine, guide the needle into the first mesh, and bring the bobbin thread to the top of the canvas to prevent threads from jamming. Let the needle swing across to the fourth open mesh and back again. Hold the canvas stationary for several stitches, allowing threads to build up on its surface. This is called bar-tacking and gives the canvas a texture and dimension similar to bargello done by hand.

Once you have the feel of this technique and the tension of the stitches is adjusted correctly, practice the "domes-and-spires" pattern as shown on the chair seat. To make the second bar tack, place the needle into the next row *and two meshes away* from the first set of stitches. Continue bar-tacking, following the pattern to the end of the row. Place the zig-zag setting on "0" and sew several up-and-down stitches along the side of the bar tacks to secure them to the canvas. Without this step, the line of stitching would unravel. You might want to try several more rows of practice stitching before moving on. To do this, change thread colors for each row. (Always use white thread in the bobbin.)

To begin working the chair seat, study the pattern at left and the sample piece you have just stitched. Using the pattern as a stitch guide and reference, count the canvas meshes so the peak of the bargello design (the highest point) falls along the top edge of the outline you have drawn on the canvas. Choose a starting point close to one edge of the canvas and start stitching at the widest end, always moving the needle from side to side, as shown in the close-up photographs, opposite.

Place the needle in the first mesh and move it across to the fourth mesh so the stitch covers three threads of canvas. (Every stitch in the design will be the same size.) Bar-tack across these four meshes to allow threads to build up on the canvas surface (as on your practice piece), going back and forth about five times so the canvas is completely covered.

For the next bar tack, carefully place your needle in the next row, *two meshes away from* the first set of bar tacks (as for the practice piece) and continue placing the needle and bar-tacking (following the pattern at left) until one row of bargello is complete. Be sure the stitching extends ½ inch beyond the actual size of the chair seat to allow a margin when turning the edges under.

At both ends of every row, place the zig-zag setting on "0" (for straight stitching) and sew several up-and-down stitches along the side of the bar tacks to help secure them (as you did for the practice piece). This is an important step since without it, your stitches will ravel and pull out.

The color sequence of the chair seat is: purple, dark blue, light blue, olive green, yellow, and gold. To begin the second row, change the

To form the pattern, bar-tack across four meshes on wide zig-zag.

Change the color of the thread before beginning each new row.

Here's what you need to "needlepoint" with a zig-zag sewing machine.

purple thread to dark blue and work row 2 as for row 1. Change colors each time you start a new row.

Continue in this way, stitching one row of color at a time, until the bargello is complete. If necessary, block the canvas following the directions on page 9.

Cut a ⅜-inch piece of plywood to fit the chair seat dimensions exactly and place a layer of quilt batting on top of the board. Place the finished canvas on top of the batting, right side up, and turn all three layers over. Secure the canvas to the backing board using a staple gun or tacks and pulling tightly along each side. Clip corners where necessary to make the canvas lie as flat as possible. Treat the bargello with a light coat of soil-retardant spray and have the piece dry-cleaned when necessary.

Metal Threads and Inlays: Bargello Pillow and Box

Needlepoint is more than just applying yarn to canvas; it can involve many different materials as well, like the metallic threads and decorative stones used in this project. The pillow and box shown at right use both of these creative materials to make two otherwise ordinary projects into something special.

The bargello pillow, backed with gold lamé, is worked in horizontal rows starting with a row of flame-shaped lozenges along the top. The box is worked in an abstract design using mother-of-pearl stones and gold and silver threads.

All of the stitches are listed in the Glossary on pages 93 to 96 and patterns are on pages 66 and 67.

Pillow
Materials
20x24 inches #18-count mono canvas
3-ply Paternayan Persian wool, or a suitable substitute, in the following colors and amounts (in yards): #010 eggshell (11), #168 light gray (6), #020 pink-beige (4), #464 peach (4), #592 pale green (2), #537 mint green (2), #B42 blue (2), #166 medium gray (3), #620 light lavender (3), and #017 light gray (1)
#3 DMC pearl cotton embroidery thread in the following colors and amounts (in yards): #3033 eggshell (6), #677 yellow (2), #3 snow white (6), #415 light gray (3), and #554 lavender (4)
6-strand DMC cotton embroidery floss in the following colors and amounts (in yards): #3023 gray-brown (2), #676 pale gold (2), #415 light gray (2), #301 light gray (2), and #318 dark gray (3)
10 yards gold cloisonné thread
14 yards silver cloisonné thread
#22 tapestry needle
Masking tape
20x24 inches gold lamé fabric
Waterproof pen
Pillow stuffing

Directions
Bind the edges of the canvas with masking tape to prevent raveling and mount the canvas in a needlepoint frame, if desired. With a waterproof marking pen, draw a two-inch border around the canvas.

Begin stitching the pillow by working the flame-shaped lozenges along the top of the pillow. The lower edge of the lozenge establishes the key line for the remainder of the pillow; all subsequent rows are worked in the same pattern using different colors.

The upper edge of the lozenge is a reverse of the key line; rows stitched above the lozenges to the top edge of the pillow (approximately one inch) follow the same pattern.

Starting at the marked line at the top right side of the pillow, count down 24 threads to begin stitching the top of the lozenge. Follow the diagram on page 66 and begin at the point marked "start." Each stitch should cover four threads on the canvas. Do not pull the yarn or thread too tightly because doing so will expose the canvas underneath and the yarn will not cover completely.

When working with wool, separate strands into individual plies; use two plies for stitching. When working with floss, use six strands. Cut wool into 18-inch lengths, and metallic threads into 10- to 12-inch lengths so they do not become worn-looking from being pulled through the canvas an excessive number of times.

When working with cloisonné thread, be careful strands do not tangle or knot. Apply beeswax to ends to keep them from unraveling. (If cloisonné twists or ravels, it will not cover canvas completely.)

Following the diagram, work the first row in gold cloisonné. Repeat the row seven more times across the canvas, for a total of eight flame-shaped lozenges. Be careful to work the center stitch only once between each of the lozenges.

After working the top of the lozenge, work the remainder of the motif inside the outlines, as indicated on the pattern. Fill centers of the lozenges with varying colors and threads, as indicated on the color key with the pattern (see page 66).

continued

Metal Threads and Inlays: Bargello Pillow and Box *(continued)*

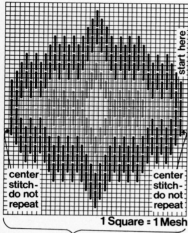

start here

center stitch- do not repeat

center stitch- do not repeat

1 Square = 1 Mesh

keyline repeat

Color and Thread Key: Pillow

Except when indicated, stitch one row in each of the following colors and threads:
1. Eggshell pearl cotton
2. Eggshell wool
3. Lavender pearl cotton
4. Light lavender wool
5. Silver cloisonné
6. Dark gray floss
7. Light gray pearl cotton
8. Medium gray wool
9. Light gray wool
10. Silver cloisonné
11. Light gray floss
12. Blue wool
13. Snow white pearl cotton (two rows)
14. Eggshell wool
15. Snow white pearl cotton
16. Pink-beige wool
17. Light gray wool
18. Mint green wool
19. Pale green wool
20. Pale gold floss
21. Gold cloisonné
22. Yellow pearl cotton
23. Peach wool
24. Gray-brown floss
25. Pink-beige wool
26. Eggshell pearl cotton
27. Light gray wool
28. Gold cloisonné

To fill the canvas between the top of the lozenge and the top (straight) edge of the pillow, start with the row of stitches immediately above the lozenge and work one row with eggshell wool. Work the next row, above it, with eggshell pearl cotton. Work the row above that with light gray wool, and fill the remaining empty rows with silver cloisonné. As you near the top of the pillow, make stitches shorter to compensate for the straight edge (so the stitches end in a straight line).

Work the first row below the gold cloisonné key line in pink-beige wool, using two strands. Work all remaining rows below the key line following the color and yarn sequence listed in the chart at left. Work the sequence approximately 2½ times, or until the pillow is 20 inches long.

Block the finished pillow following the directions on page 9. Then trim the two-inch border of unworked canvas to ½ inch. Cut two pieces of muslin the same size as the trimmed canvas and stitch them into a pillow form. Stuff and slip-stitch the opening. Then cut a piece of gold lamé to size and finish the pillow, following the directions on page 28.

Accent the lower edge of the pillow with seven tassels made from leftover yarn. For each tassel, wrap eggshell and beige yarns and threads 20 times or more around a 2½-inch piece of cardboard. Tie strands tightly together, leaving the ends of the tying strand four inches long. Clip loops.

Wrap leftover colored threads around the top of the tassel to a depth of about ⅝ inch, and thread the ends of the wrapping thread through to the inside of the tassel. Add gold and silver accents, if desired. Stitch to the pillow as shown in the photograph.

Box
Materials
3-ply Paternayan Persian wool yarn, or a similar substitute, in the following colors and amounts (in yards): #137 purple (9), #758 blue (2), #592 green (6), #464 peach (5), #014 off-white (5), and #015 pale yellow (6)
7 yards #3 white pearl cotton
8 yards gold cloisonné thread
8 yards silver cloisonné thread
11x13-inches #10-count canvas
1½x1⅞-inch mother-of-pearl shell
5 small pearl-like stones
3½x6x9-inch wooden box with 5¾x8¾-inch recessed top (see note below)
#18 tapestry needle
Masking tape
Waterproof marking pen
Quilt batting or mat board
White glue

Directions
Note: The finished size of this design is 8¾x5¾ inches (to fit inside a recessed top the same size). If you need to adjust the finished size, extend the design lines or add a border to make the design larger. Or, use a smaller scale when enlarging the pattern to make the finished design smaller.

Tape edges of canvas. Enlarge the pattern opposite, following directions on page 42, and trace it onto canvas with a waterproof pen. Center the design so there are at least two inches of unworked canvas on all sides. The entire design is worked in basket-weave stitches except where otherwise noted. Use full three-ply strands of Persian wool yarn, and refer to the Glossary on pages 93 to 96 for how-to instructions.

Work all of the basket-weave areas, referring to the pattern for colors and to the Glossary for stitch how-to. When working

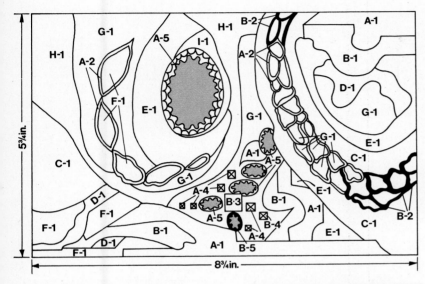

Color and Stitch Key: Box

Gold—A
Silver—B
Purple—C
Blue—D
Green—E
Peach—F
Off-white—G
Pale yellow—H
White pearl cotton—I

Basket-weave stitch—1
Chain stitch—2
Triple cross-stitch—3
Cross-stitch—4
Buttonhole stitch—5

with the cloisonné thread, cut short pieces so they are less likely to tangle or knot. Apply beeswax to the ends to keep the pieces from unraveling. Do not let the thread become twisted or it will not cover the canvas.

Next, fill remaining areas in chain, triple-cross-, and cross-stitches. (Refer to the Glossary for stitch how-to.) Do not work the canvas under the stones.

Glue each stone in place on the canvas, using white glue that dries transparent; let dry. Sew the stones in place (using gold or silver cloisonné) one at a time, using a buttonhole stitch around the edges, as shown in the diagram at right. Pull the loops tightly, adding another row of stitches inside the first row until the stones are secure.

Block as instructed on page 9 and trim the unworked canvas to within ½ inch of the finished edges. Turn under the unworked canvas and glue to the back. Cut a piece of quilt batting or mat board to fit under the needlepoint and glue the entire finished piece to the recessed area in the top of the box.

Securing Stones to Canvas

To secure the stones to the needlepoint, first glue them in place on the canvas; let glue dry thoroughly. Then, using either gold or silver cloisonné (as indicated on the color key) bring the needle up at 1 (see diagram). Go down at 2, leaving a small, fairly tight loop on top of the stone. Bring the needle up at 3 and down at 4. Repeat this procedure until you have made a complete circle around each stone.

Begin the second round by bringing the needle up and over the first loop (formed by stitch 1-2), making a detached buttonhole stitch. Then take the next stitch over the second loop (stitch 3-4); pull fairly tightly, drawing the stitches closer to the center of the stones. Continue around, making detached buttonhole stitches over the loops formed by the first round of stitches. End the thread on the back side of the canvas.

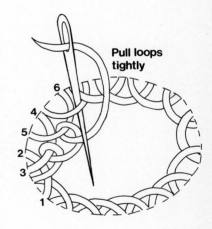

Pull loops tightly

Raffia Stitchery—Bargello Baskets

Exciting new materials are available for needlepoint! These stunning contemporary baskets, for example, are bargello-stitched in sleek Swistraw ribbon on sturdy but flexible plastic canvas.

Materials
10½x13½-inch sheets Columbia Minerva plastic mesh
Tapestry needle
Waterproof marking pen

Cylinder
2 sheets plastic mesh
One 24-yard skein matte-finish Swistraw in each of the following colors: powder blue, purple, lemon yellow, medium blue, hot pink, and orange

Octagon
3 sheets plastic mesh
Two 24-yard skeins brilliant-finish Swistraw in each of the following colors: canary yellow, rose, vermilion, lime green, turquoise, and purple

Cube
3 sheets plastic mesh
One 24-yard skein brilliant-finish Swistraw in each of the following colors: lavender, medium blue, champagne, and salmon

General Directions
Cut plastic mesh, following the directons below. If measurement falls between meshes, extend it to the next solid line.

Cut 60-inch pieces of Swistraw; use doubled. Begin in lower left corner except for cube, which begins in the center.

On charts at right, each grid line equals a plastic filament;

each square equals one mesh.

Join pieces by overcasting with matching Swistraw.

Cylinder: Cut two 4½-inch-wide mesh strips; join into a 4½x18-inch strip. (Overlap the two strips by four meshes; sew together with Swistraw.) Work the cylinder in rows of flame stitches across the width. Each stitch covers five "threads."

Hold the strip with a 4½-inch end closest to you and begin an inch above the edge. Stitch as shown in the photograph. Work each row the same as the first one. When one inch from the end, join the strip into a circle by overlapping the ends three meshes. Adjust stitch length.

For the base, cut a 5½-inch circle; join every third mesh.

Octagon: Cut eight 6¾x3½-inch rectangles; complete one panel using the chart at right. Work variations for the next seven panels, studying the photograph to see how color bars extend from panel to panel.

Take stitches over edges of meshes at top only; at other edges, leave one line of plastic unstitched. Join panels.

Cut an eight-sided figure, 3½ inches per side, and join it to the panels along the bottom.

Cube: Cut five squares of meshes, about 40 meshes each (six inches). Following the chart at right, stitch four sides. (The chart shows the upper right quarter of each side; repeat to complete each side.)

Begin by making a small cross-stitch in the center of the square and working out. Vary color combinations on each side. Take stitches over edge of meshes. Join the four sides. For the base, trim one line of plastic on two adjacent edges of the fifth square. Stitch base to sides and corners.

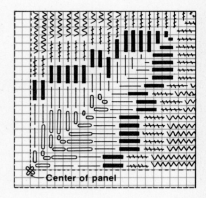

Center of panel

color 1   color 2   color 3
color 4   color 5

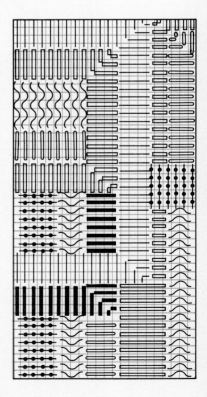

Yellow   Lime   Rose
Blue   Orange   Purple

Free-Form Stitchery

Create your own free-form needlepoint piece and let your imagination guide you through a galaxy of ideas, colors, and stitches. If you clip and turn the edges of your canvas, you can achieve wonderful outlines and curves, as in our example at right.

If you're stuck for design ideas, just take a favorite object, make an abstract drawing of it, and transfer the drawing to canvas. Follow the general instructions at right, but use your imagination to come up with a truly unique needlepoint creation. No pattern is given, so colors and shapes are left entirely to you.

Materials
Needlepoint canvas
Scraps of yarn in assorted
  colors
Tapestry needle
Graph paper
Waterproof marking pen
Colored pencils

Directions
The abstract needlepoint piece shown opposite is meant to be a one-of-a-kind design. When planning and stitching your own free-form sampler, use our piece for ideas, but keep your design creative and original. Refer to the photograph for color and placement ideas, if desired, but draw an original pattern incorporating your own ideas and preferences into the design.

Our sampler is approximately 5x11 inches and is worked on a single piece of #12-count canvas. Feel free to make your design any size and to stitch it on the canvas of your choice. You can use purchased canvas, a scrap left from a previous project, or even several scraps in different sizes joined together as a ground for your creative stitchery.

Before you begin stitching, plan your design on paper. Here are several useful design techniques. The first could be called the "paper dolls" technique. Cut out various leaves, triangles, or other shapes that appeal to you. Arrange them on paper and then trace around them. Leave the outline of the design irregular, rather than placing the shapes in a box or frame. With this type of designing, the trick is to look not only at the shapes, but also at the background areas. These are called "negative spaces" and should be as pleasingly arranged as the objects themselves.

If abstractions appeal to you, try designing with cut or torn paper. Take a sheet of paper and cut or tear it into large and small fragments. Arrange these on the paper until both the shapes and the negative spaces please you. If the paper forms are cut from different colored tissue paper, their overlappings may suggest color schemes. Or, sketch an abstract shape by closing your eyes and "scribbling" with a pencil on a piece of paper. Open your eyes and evaluate your "design." If necessary, divide the shape into a number of smaller shapes.

Fill each section of your design with colored pencils, making a pleasant color arrangement. Or, using a pencil for shading, divide the design into light, medium, and dark areas. Plan to put your strongest colors in the heavily shaded areas and the palest colors in the lightly shaded areas. You may wish to leave some spaces open for needle weaving or drawn-thread work.

While the design is still on paper, consider variations in the texture of your stitchery and note those areas that are to be relatively smooth and flat (worked in tent stitches, for example) and those that are to have more texture and dimension (worked in crossed or knotted stitches, for example).

When you're pleased with the overall design, transfer the general outlines to canvas, following the directions on page 10. Work sections in a variety of colors and stitches, using the paper pattern as a guide. Combine cutwork and pulled-thread work to give your design see-through areas, as shown in the photograph.

When the sampler is complete, block gently and trim the edges of the canvas to within ½ inch of the stitching. Turn under the ½-inch margin and press, clipping where necessary and tacking to hold in place. Back with a piece of fabric, if desired. (Be sure to cut holes in the backing fabric to allow light to show through the cut areas.)

Display your original free-form stitchery in a standing frame made with sheets of clear acrylic, if desired.

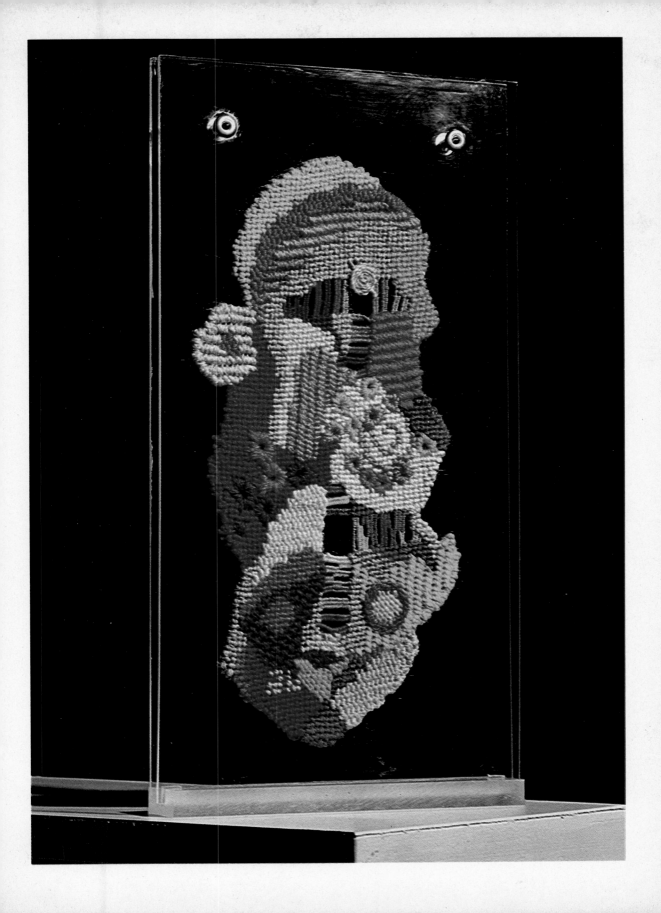

Spectacular Stitchery

Art from Your Needle

Using yarn on canvas the way an artist uses paint on canvas, you can create beautiful needlepoint designs like the fishpond rug shown here. The projects in this section are masterpieces of color and pattern. Although each one demands a good deal of time, the results are well worth the effort—needlepoint stitchery like this is a joy forever. To create this very special fishpond rug with intricate petit-point detailing, please turn the page.

Fishpond Rug *(shown on pages 72 and 73)*

This rug comes alive with subtly-shaded flora and petit-point fauna. Create special effects by blending contrasting colors of wool, and using cotton floss for shimmery highlights on the goldfish.

Refer to the outline pattern and closeup photographs on the following pages for color and shading details.

Materials

1½ yards (36-inch-wide) #10/20-count penelope canvas
3-ply Persian wool (see note)
Cotton embroidery floss (see note)
#18 tapestry needle
#24 tapestry needle
Four yards bias tape
Waterproof marking pen
Fabric for backing, if desired

Directions

Note: You will need 3-ply Persian yarn in white, black, gray, dark yellow, goldenrod, medium and dark bittersweet, light tangerine, light and dark salmon, orange, melon, light silver, light sand, pale russet, sapphire, pale blue, pale and light beige, lilac, and ice green. You will also need varying shades — from light to dark — of loden green, olive green, dark olive, spruce green, lime green, and bronze green. The background is worked in combinations of medium-olive and medium-bronze greens, and requires approximately 400 yards of each color. In addition, you will need cotton floss for the petit-point animals in colors shown in the photograph.

Enlarge the outline pattern on page 75 according to the directions on page 42. Transfer the pattern to the canvas with a waterproof marking pen, leaving a three-inch margin all around. If desired, mount the canvas in a frame to prevent warping.

Needlepoint the design, using the photographs, pattern, and these directions as a guide. Feel free to make changes or modifications in the colors to match your decorating scheme.

Lily Pads: The rounded lily pad shapes are worked in basket-weave stitches with three strands of Persian wool and a #18 tapestry needle. Referring to the pattern and photograph, work the lily pads in shades of green. Note that several pads are shaded on the pattern, indicating they are "below" the water's surface, or in shadow. Work these pads in the darkest shades of green, or in blends of green and another color, such as rust. (To blend a color, simply replace one strand of yarn with a contrasting strand.) Work the pads "floating" on the water in shades of bright light green, with accents of yellow or blue-green so they show up more clearly.

Water Lilies: Refer to the pattern for outline and positioning of water lilies, and to the closeup photo for color and shading. Work the flowers in continental stitches (see directions on pages 93 to 96). If desired, add French knots for flower centers.

Background: Begin filling background in upper right corner of rug with basket-weave stitches. To achieve the striated effect, blend olive and bronze greens as for shaded areas of lily pads, alternating the dominant color. Be sure to leave areas for the petit-point figures as shown in the outline pattern.

Goldfish, Frog, Butterfly: Work the figures in petit point (see directions on page 75) using a #24 tapestry needle. Refer to the closeup photograph on page 77 and to the chart to work the first goldfish. Work all other fish with similar shading, and other figures according to the photographs. Use floss to create shimmery areas on figures; use two or more shades of floss for shading.

Spider, Web, Butterfly Detail: For spider, embroider body and legs with short satin stitches using one strand of black wool. For web, combine two strands white floss and one strand green floss; lay on canvas in the position shown on the pattern. Couch floss to canvas with short stitches every ¼ inch. Couch each strand of the web; couch brown floss similarly for butterfly antennae.

To finish, block the rug (see directions on page 9). For edges, trim excess canvas from rug, leaving a ½-inch margin. Stitch bias tape to canvas edge and fold under. Tack other edge to canvas, tucking tape along curves so rug will lie flat. If desired, blindstitch a fabric backing to reverse side of rug for protection. Shake the rug to remove loose dirt particles. Dry-clean when necessary.

Butterfly

Fish

—Fish

Fish

Frog

1 Square = 2 Inches

Petit Point

Petit point is a means of adding more detail to needlepoint projects, since it is worked on canvas that yields 18 or more stitches per inch. Mono canvas with 18, 20, or 22 stitches per inch (and finer) is suitable for small projects that are worked entirely in petit point. Penelope canvas, however, is recommended for projects with a combination of both petit point and larger needlepoint stitches, and it has a distinctive double-thread weave. To work petit point on penelope canvas, just separate the threads with the tip of your needle, and work four tiny stitches where just one larger needlepoint stitch would have been. Work petit point with one strand of Persian wool or several strands of embroidery floss. Whichever you use, make sure that the fiber is neither so thick that it distorts the canvas, nor so thin that the canvas threads show through.

continued

Fishpond Rug *(continued)*

M   Lt. Tangerine
| Orange
/   Pale Beige
o   Dk. Bittersweet
人   Autumn
▶   Med. Melon
>   Bright Pink
•   Med. Rust
—   Yellow-gold floss
+   Lt. Pink floss

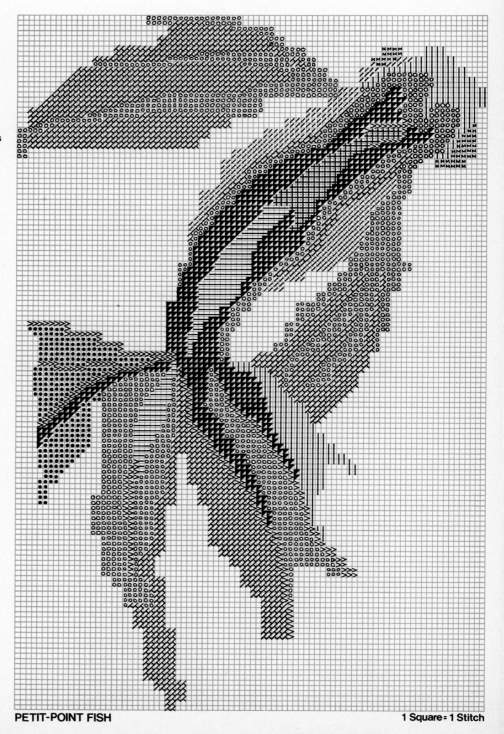

PETIT-POINT FISH   1 Square = 1 Stitch

Della Robbia Wreath

All the color and glory of a traditional Della Robbia wreath are captured in this beautiful needlepoint creation.

The wreath, stitched entirely in continental stitches, is worked one section of color at a time. Work directly from the pattern on pages 80 and 81, repeating the pattern four times to complete the wreath.

Mount the finished needlepoint on a plywood board, adding layers of quilt batting for dimension.

Materials

3-ply Paternayan yarn, or a similar substitute, in the amounts (32-inch strands) and colors on pages 80 and 81
24x24 inches #14-count canvas
Eight to twelve #19 tapestry needles
24x24 inches ⅜-inch plywood
Compass (for drawing circles)
Waterproof marking pen
Quilt batting
20x20 inches green felt
4-inch-wide red velvet ribbon
Masking tape
Staple gun

Directions

Bind the edges of the canvas with masking tape to prevent raveling, and draw an 18-inch circle in the middle of the canvas using a compass and waterproof pen. Divide the circle into fourths and draw a 7-inch circle in the center of the 18-inch circle. The small circle is the center of the wreath and will not be filled in. Wait until the needlepoint is complete before cutting out the center circle.

Count the squares from the inside edge to the outside of the wreath to make sure they equal the number on the graph (pages 80 and 81). Adjust the size of the circle so it corresponds to the number of squares on the graph, if necessary.

Add an extra ½ inch (about 7 spaces) to the inner and outer edges of the graph and the circle on the canvas. These spaces will be filled with additional white yarn to match the background so that when the wreath is cut and turned, none of the design will be lost.

Soak the yarn in cold water for three to five minutes to remove any color residue and to make sure the colors do not run. Gently squeeze out excess moisture and lay the yarn flat to dry. (Do not dry the yarn in direct sunlight.) Be sure the yarn dries thoroughly before you begin stitching.

Separate strands into individual plies, and use two plies for stitching. Begin stitching one quadrant of the wreath, following the graph on the following pages. The entire wreath is done in continental stitches (see the Glossary on pages 93 to 96). Work one section of color, carry the yarn to the back, and leave it long and threaded on the needle (rather than ending or cutting it) so that when you need the same color again, you will not have to re-thread a new strand. If the long yarns get in your way while stitching, pull them to one side and tape them to the canvas.

When you finish one quadrant, label one end of the pattern A and the other end B. To begin work in the second quadrant, match end B of the first quadrant to end A of the second and begin stitching. Continue in this way until all four sections are complete. Work the white background as you go, filling in the extra ½ inch along the inside and outside edges.

Block the wreath according to the directions on page 9. Since the entire wreath is done in continental stitches, it may be necessary to block the canvas twice. Cut around the wreath shape and the inside circle, leaving two inches of unworked canvas along both inside and outside edges.

Cut a 17¼-inch circle from the plywood board and sand the rough edges until they are smooth. Then, cut a 6½-inch circle from the center of the large plywood circle and sand the edges.

Cut three layers of quilt batting to match the size of the plywood. With the batting as padding, lay the wreath on top of the plywood and staple the canvas to the back of the board, pulling the edges tightly. Clip curves when necessary to make edges lie flat and to eliminate puckering.

Cut a piece of green felt to match the plywood and glue it (with a light, even coat of white glue) to the back of the wreath, covering the canvas edges. Let the glue dry thoroughly.

Tie a bow with 4-inch-wide red velvet ribbon and tack the bow in place at the bottom of the wreath, making sure it is secure. Trim the ends of the bow as desired.

continued

Della Robbia Wreath *(continued)*

Color		Symbol				
R 70 Light holly (9 strands)		L	G 54 Med. green (19	"	)	+
R 10 Dark holly (9	")	/	504 Dark green (35	"	)	◤
010 White (45	")	□	865 Light golden red (6	"	)	—
G 74 Pale green (11	")	○	855 Light red (8	"	)	•
G 64 Light green (20	")	M	845 Med. red (20	"	)	▲
			810 Dark red (24	"	)	×

This pattern is for one quadrant (one quarter) of the wreath design. To complete the quadrant, fit together the two halves of the pattern along the notched edge down the center of each page.

975 Pale orange (5   "   )   T
965 Light orange (10   "   )   =
960 Med. orange (7   "   )   ●
958 Dark orange (7   "   )   ■
528 Dark blue green (6   "   )   ▪
532 Med. blue green (6   "   )   ‖

535 Light blue green (4   "   )   z
113 Dark brown (24   "   )   ■
405 Med. brown (12   "   )   ●
420 Light brown (10   "   )   /
430 Pale brown (12   "   )   ·
433 Dark yellow (gold) (12   "   )   ◢

427 Med. yellow (13   "   )   ✕
441 Light lemon yellow (17   "   )   —
437 Pale lemon yellow (17   "   )   ○
590 Light olive green (11   "   )   /
553 Med. olive green (8   "   )   ◢
540 Dark olive green (9   "   )   ■

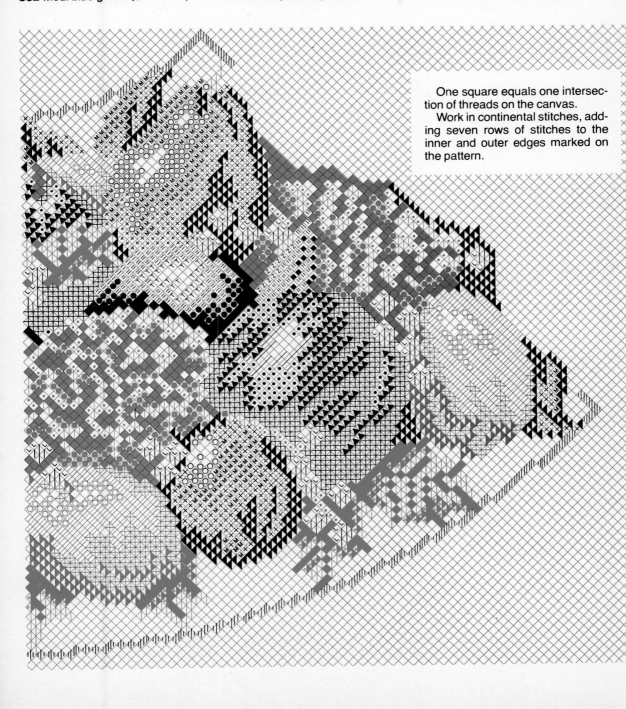

One square equals one intersection of threads on the canvas.
Work in continental stitches, adding seven rows of stitches to the inner and outer edges marked on the pattern.

Needlepoint Crèche

Christmas manger scenes have spanned many centuries and cultures. Our stately crèche figures are a happy combination of old-world expressiveness and contemporary geometrics.

Although there are a variety of color combinations, the use of a single stitch – the continental stitch – keeps the project simple. Patterns for the figures are on pages 84 to 87.

Materials

3-ply Persian wool in the colors and amounts listed on the chart on page 84
1⅔ yards 36-inch mono canvas (12 or 14 meshes per inch) (See note.)
#17 tapestry needle
9x12-inch felt pieces in the following amounts and colors: 1 orange, 1 yellow, 1 turquoise, and 2 navy blue
8½-inch piece of ¹⁄₁₆-inch-diameter brass wire for staff
24-inch piece of ¹⁄₃₂-inch-diameter aluminum wire for angel wings
Lightweight cardboard
White glue
Shredded foam or cotton batting for stuffing
Waterproof pen
1-inch masking tape

Directions

Note: To reduce warping and buckling of completed needlepoint, you may wish to substitute interlock for mono canvas. In addition, interlock won't ravel when trimmed, so you need not apply white glue to the edges of the completed needlepoint.

Enlarge the patterns on the following pages according to the directions on page 42. Cut the canvas pieces two inches larger on all sides than the patterns show, and bind raw edges with masking tape. Position canvas pieces over the enlarged patterns, leaving two inches of canvas all around and making sure that the horizontal and vertical threads of the canvas run square to the facial detail. Trace the outlines with a waterproof pen. As an alternative, do not cut the canvas pieces apart, but transfer up to four patterns to one large piece of canvas. Mount in a working frame, and stitch all the figures at once.

Using two strands of the three-ply wool and following color key on page 84, work the figures entirely in continental stitches. Begin and end threads with waste knots. Begin with facial details and work all areas of one color with the same length of yarn. For example, work Joseph's forehead, cheeks, eyelids, and chin in white before working other facial details. Then fill in hair and body areas. Go ahead and assemble this figure, or wait and assemble the entire crèche at once. Block if necessary.

To assemble, carefully apply a thin line of glue ⅛ inch from the edge of the completed needlepoint around all sides and allow to dry. This glue prevents raveling (if you are using interlock canvas, eliminate this gluing step). Trim around needlepoint ¼ inch from all outside edges, being careful not to cut into glue or stitches. To give the head its rounded shape, make a ⅜-inch-deep cut into each V at top of figure. Fold Vs inward (making a dart) and stitch together with one strand of the same color yarn as used in adjoining needlepoint. Close back seam similarly.

Turn figure upside down and stuff. For bottom, trace and cut cardboard oval to fit; cut felt oval also, adding ¼ inch margin to cardboard pattern. Glue cardboard, centered, to felt oval. Allow to dry. Position felt bottom on inverted figure (with cardboard to the inside), and tuck the extra felt to the inside. Using one strand of yarn, sew felt bottom to the edge of the figure, keeping raw edges of felt and canvas inside.

For halos, glue and trim around edges of needlepoint halos as for the figures. Fold under raw edges and glue. Cut matching halo from felt; glue lightly to back of needlepoint halos. If desired, place a stack of books or other heavy objects on halo to keep it flat until glue dries. Stitch together edges of felt and needlepoint. Using one strand of matching yarn, attach halo to head.

Glue and trim angel wings as for halos. Fold under raw edges of canvas. Before gluing them down permanently, cut aluminum wire to fit around outer edges of wings for stiffening. Bend wire to match outline of wings. Position shaped wire inside folded-under canvas edges; glue edges down. Cut felt to fit wings. Stitch together felt and needlepoint and attach wings to angel.

For shepherd's staff, cut an 8½-inch piece of brass wire, and bend into shape as shown on the pattern. Attach to hand section of shepherd with matching yarn.

continued

Needlepoint Crèche *(continued)*

Color Key

You may use yarn in the colors listed below, or see the note on page 86 for alternatives.

Color	Number	Yards
White	1	15
Pink	2	8
Light fuchsia	3	14
Magenta	4	5
Bright red	5	10
Deep red	6	4
Crimson red	7	6
Vermillion	8	4
Light orange	9	12
Orange	10	12
Burnt orange	11	30
Pale yellow	12	2
Light yellow	13	5
Yellow	14	6
Golden yellow	15	2
Yellow-gold	16	4
Gold	17	12
Yellow-ocher	18	26
Light olive	19	2
Olive	20	18
Light blue-green	21	12
Medium blue-green	22	15
Dark blue-green	23	10
Light blue	24	5
Sky blue	25	8
Light true blue	26	18
Medium blue	27	10
True blue	28	5
Royal blue	29	19
Heather blue	30	16
Dark heather blue	31	10
Navy blue	32	24
Dark navy blue	33	5
Pale lavender-blue	34	2
Light lavender-blue	35	12
Lavender-blue	36	26
Lavender	37	14
Red-violet	38	10
Dark purple	39	10
Light tan	40	2
Tan	41	12
Burnt sienna	42	13

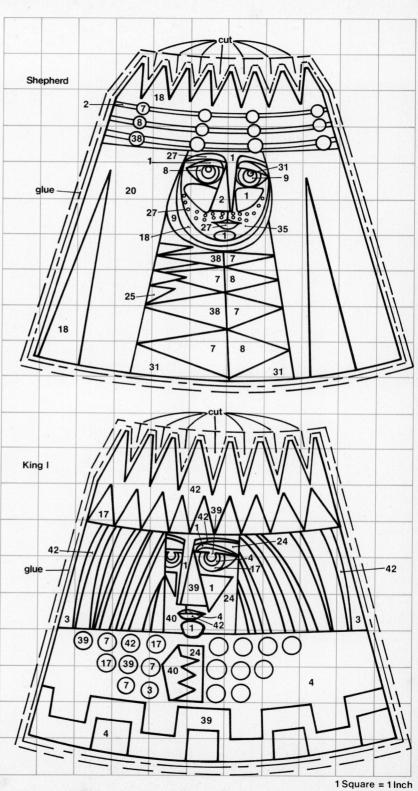

1 Square = 1 Inch

85

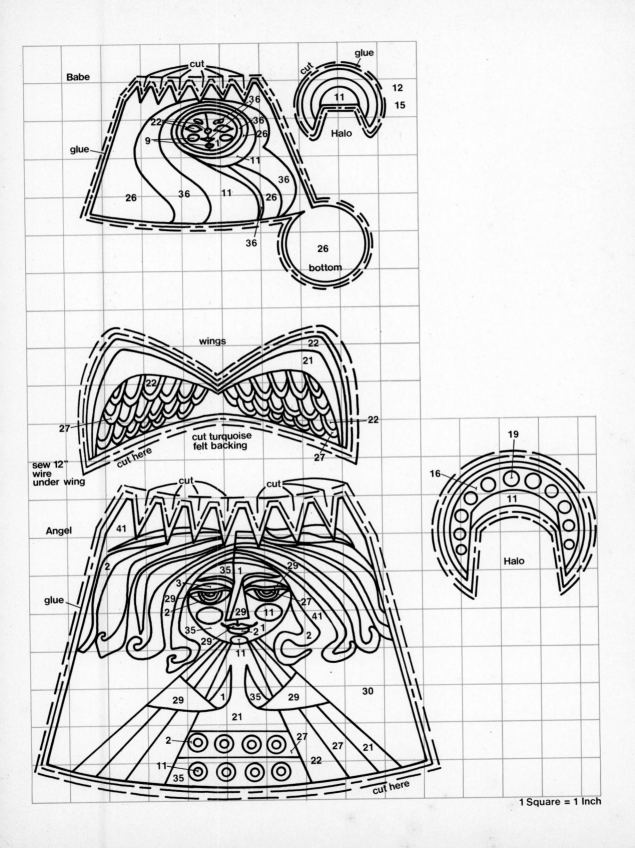

1 Square = 1 Inch

Needlepoint Crèche *(continued)*

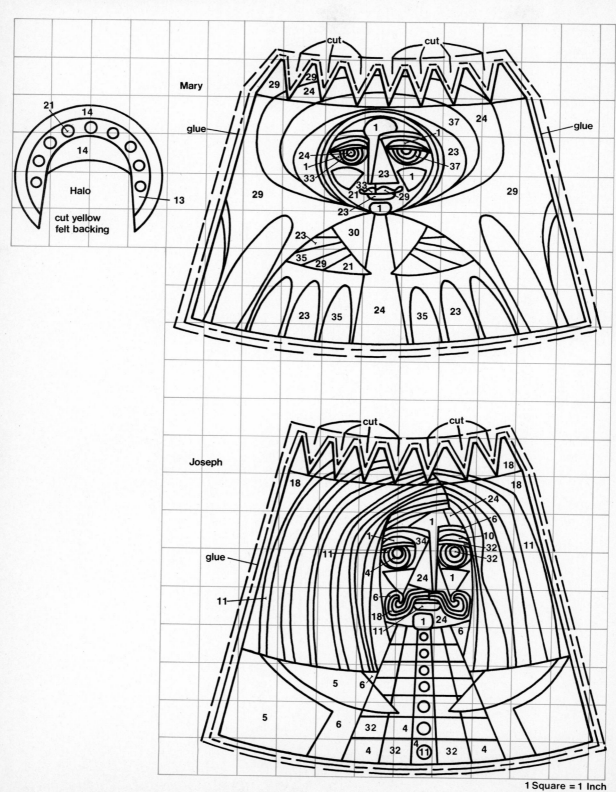

Mary

Halo

21
14
14
13

cut yellow
felt backing

cut   cut

29   29
24

glue

1
37   24
1
24
23
1
37
33
23   1
21   33
29
23   1

glue

29

29

23
30
35
29   21
23   35   24   35   23

cut   cut

Joseph

18

18
18
18

glue

11

11

1
24
6
10
32
32
11

1
34
11
4
24   1
6
18
11
1   24
6

5   6
5
6   32   4
4   32   4   11   32   4

1 Square = 1 Inch

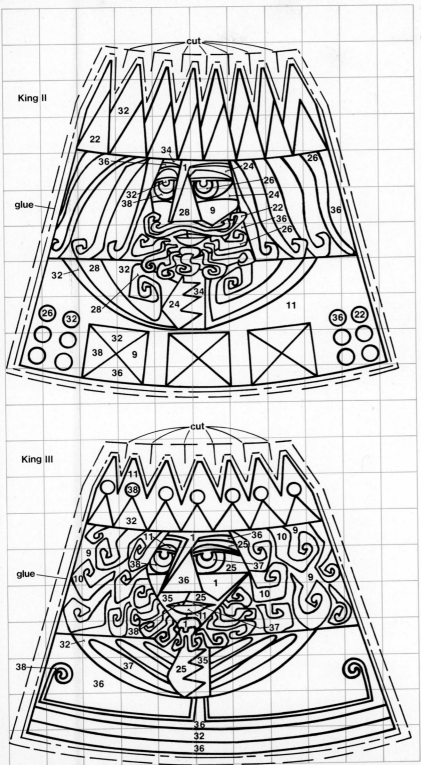

1 Square = 1 Inch

Creating Color Schemes

In this needlepoint project, rich hues and lustrous tonal values are achieved by using many shades of several basic colors. If you are unable to locate all the shades listed, or don't wish to purchase an entire skein to obtain the small amount of necessary yarn, you can make substitutions. For example, you could use lavender-blue throughout instead of buying additional shades of pale lavender-blue and light lavender-blue. Or, you may wish to use up small quantities of Persian yarn left over from previous needlepoint projects. When you make *any* yarn substitution on a project involving small-scale stitches, remember to strive for overall color impact. A good test of color compatibility is to stand back and squint at the proposed colors: if the "blur" looks good to you, any positioning of the colors in the groups will be successful.

Soft-Sculpture Lion

*What could be more fun
than stitching the king of
beasts in needlepoint!
And Karut, our
soft-sculpture lion, is
designed to let you show
off all your stitchery skills
as well, for he's worked
in a stunning array of
stitches. Patterns for
each section of the lion
are on pages 90 to 92.*

Materials
60 inches (36-inch-wide)
  #12-count interlock canvas
⅔ yard (44-inch-wide) purple
  unclipped corduroy
3x8 inches red suede
3-ply Paternayan Persian yarn,
  or a suitable substitute, in the
  following colors and
  amounts: #321 navy (35
  yards), #114 dark brown (48),
  #145 medium brown (23),
  #893 mauve (38), #650 violet
  (31), #958 red-orange (29),
  #424 burnt orange (37), #645
  magenta (42), and #R10 red
  (3 skeins, 8 yards)
Small amounts of #3 pearl
  cotton in the following
  colors: magenta, violet, navy,
  and orange
1 skein red 6-strand cotton
  embroidery floss
3 skeins white #3 pearl cotton
4 ounces navy knitting wool
12 inches brass wire
  (¹⁄₁₆-inch-diameter) for tail
2 orange Shisha mirrors
5 yards coated electrical wire
  (¹⁄₁₆-inch-diameter) for mane
  (optional)
Navy and magenta acrylic
  paints
Paintbrush
Clear-drying white glue
Approximately 15 pounds of
  polyester stuffing
#20 tapestry needle

Directions
Enlarge the patterns on pages 90 to 92 and transfer them to canvas, following directions on pages 42 and 43. Make sure grain lines on pattern match straight grain of canvas. Do not cut out individual pattern pieces before stitching. Instead, bind edges of canvas with tape; mount canvas in a frame for stitching, if desired.

Work the lion following the color and stitch keys with the pattern. Or substitute your own colors and stitches. If you choose alternate stitches, remember that the lion is a playful piece of needle art; feel free to let your imagination roam, selecting a variety of interesting and unusual stitches from your needlepoint repertoire. Diagrams for Turkey work (the rya-knot stitch) and the Van Dyke stitch, fan stitch, and brick stitch are with the patterns. For an explanation of the remaining stitches, see pages 93 to 96.

The lion's face is worked in two pieces. The pattern is for the right side of the face; reverse it for the left side. Work tent-stitched areas first, then fill areas worked in unusual stitches. Finally, add Shisha mirrors as follows. Glue mirrors in place with white glue. When the glue dries, work five fan-shaped straight stitches across the mirror using six strands of red cotton floss (see photograph). At the end of the mirror closest to the center of the face, work five rows of plain weaving over and under the straight stitches.

The front of the body and the tops of the front legs are worked in a single piece, as are the front side and back side pieces. Note that across the front body there are four squares that spell WORK, just as PLAY and ROAR are spelled on the front side piece and LOVE on the back side piece. If desired, substitute your own words in these squares. Work tent-stitched areas first, then the fancier stitches. On the front side piece, stitch your initials in the triangle to the right of ROAR.

On the tail, work alternate squares of mauve and violet tent stitches. At end of tail, work 1½ inches of navy tent stitches, except work two rows of Turkey loops across the middle. (For how-to for Turkey loops, see page 90.) Make loops between knots approximately ½ inch long by wrapping yarn over a pencil between stitches; leave loops uncut. Finish with 1¼ inches of Turkey work at end of tail, making loops 2 inches long; cut loops open to make a row of fringe.

When all stitching is finished, block the needlepoint, if necessary, and then cut out the individual pieces for the lion, adding ¼-inch seam allowances to all edges.

To assemble the head, stitch face pieces together along center front; overcast-stitch along the seam line using yarn in appropriate colors. Fold seam margin on ears to back of needlepoint; steam-press. Glue seam allowance to the back of ears with white glue. Cut two ear shapes (without seam allowances) from red suede; glue one to back of each ear. When glue is dry, overcast-stitch suede and needlepoint ears together with magenta yarn. Paint any exposed canvas with magenta acrylic paint. Pin ears to face along marked areas, with needlepoint facing front; stitch.

Paint the head back pieces with navy blue acrylic paint. After it dries, stitch the center back seam. With right sides facing, stitch head back to front, leaving lower edge (neck) open. Turn right side out and stuff firmly. Set head aside.

continued

Soft-Sculpture Lion *(continued)*

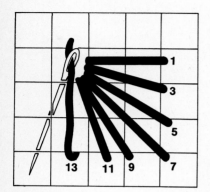

Fan Stitch

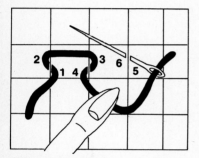

Turkey Loop Stitch

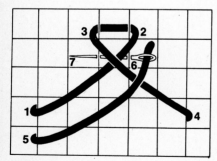

Van Dyke Stitch

For the tail, stitch the long edges together and turn the tail right side out. Sew the navy end together and stuff the tail firmly. Bend a small hook in one end of the brass wire, then insert wire in tail with hook at open end.

To assemble the body, baste the side front piece (side 1) to the front body, matching D to D. Stitch and overcast the seam, if desired, using matching yarns. Baste and stitch the side back piece (side 2) to the front body, matching B to B. Stitch the side front to side back along the top of the body, leaving an opening for the tail. Both the sides and the front are inside at this seam joining.

When adding the bottom, put the right side of the fabric inside and attach at points V, W, S, C, and A. Stitch along the edge of the needlepoint. Clip the seam allowance on the exterior curves and at A, C, S, V, and W. Leave open the spot at which the tail is to be inserted. Turn the stitched pieces and the bottom right side out and stuff tightly. At the neck opening of the body, add a line of Turkey work, making loops 1½ inches long. Clip loops. Insert tail at opening and stitch to body.

For the lion's mane, stitch knitting yarn across back of head in Turkey work, making loops about four inches long. Space rows of Turkey-work stitches about ½ inch apart. If desired, cut electrical wire into 6-inch pieces; fold pieces in half. Then cut 12-inch lengths of knitting yarn. Working with yarn in groups of three, fold yarn lengths in half and wrap or braid over doubled wire pieces. Sew covered wires to head. The wire will make the mane stand up, giving the lion a delightfully wild look. Finish by stitching the head to the body in the direction you'd like the lion to face.

continued

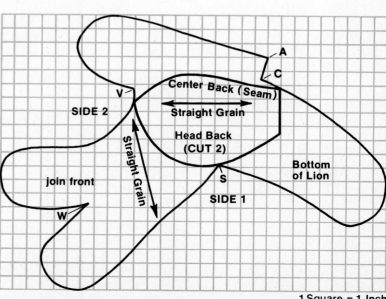

1 Square = 1 Inch

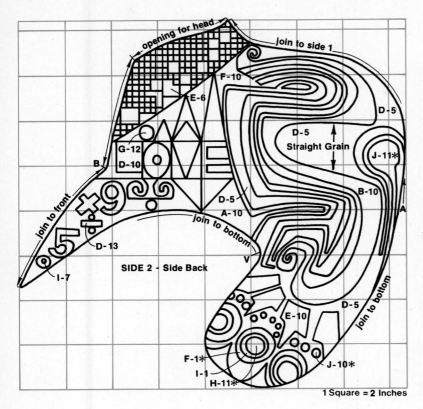

SIDE 2 - Side Back

1 Square = 2 Inches

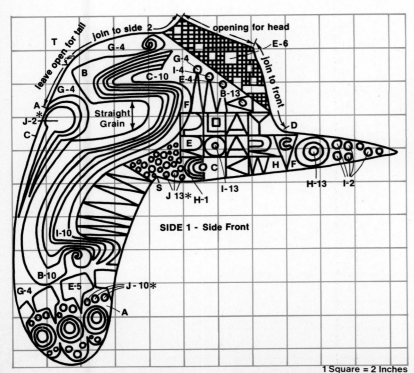

SIDE 1 - Side Front

1 Square = 2 Inches

Stitch Key
1. Chain stitch
2. Fan stitch
3. Van Dyke stitch
4. Bargello stitch
5. Brick stitch
6. Scotch stitch
7. French knot
8. Turkey loop stitch
9. Shisha mirror
10. Tent stitch
11. Fan stitch
12. Diamond eyelet stitch
13. Wheat sheaf stitch
14. Double cross-stitch
15. Upright Gobelin stitch

Color Key
A. Navy
B. Dark brown
C. Medium brown
D. Mauve
E. Violet
F. Red-orange
G. Burnt orange
H. Magenta
I. Red
J. White

*pearl cotton

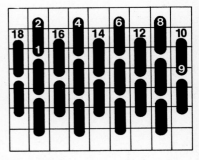

Brick Stitch

Soft-Sculpture Lion *(continued)*

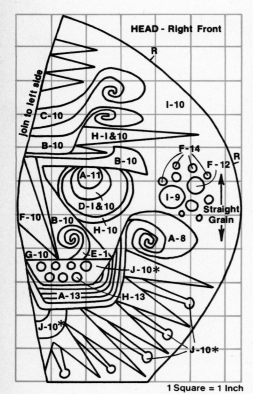

HEAD - Right Front

Join to left side

R
C-10
I-10
B-10
H-I&10
B-10
F-14
F-12
R
A-11
D-I&10
I-9
F-10
B-10
H-10
A-8
Straight Grain
G-10
E-1
J-10*
A-13
H-13
J-10*
J-10*

1 Square = 1 Inch

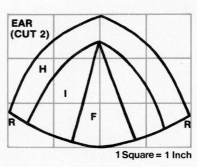

EAR (CUT 2)

H
I
F
R
R

1 Square = 1 Inch

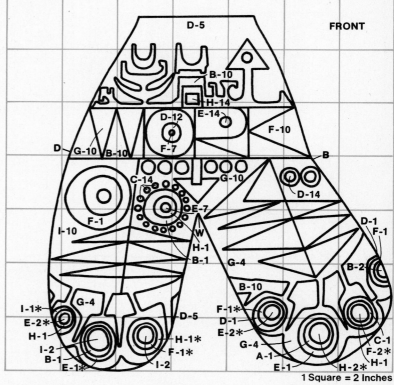

FRONT

D-5
B-10
H-14
D-12
E-14
F-7
F-10
D
G-10
B-10
B
C-14
G-10
D-14
I-10
F-1
E-7
W
H-1
B-1
G-4
B-10
D-1
F-1
B-2
I-1*
G-4
D-5
F-1*
E-2*
H-1
H-1*
D-1
E-2*
I-2
F-1*
G-4
C-1
B-1
I-2
A-1
F-2*
E-1*
E-1
H-2*
H-1

1 Square = 2 Inches

TAIL

8			E	D							
		8	D	E							T
			E	D							

1 Square = 1 Inch

Basic Needlepoint Stitches

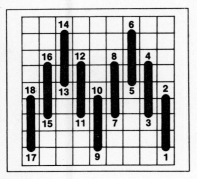

Bargello

(Also called Flame Stitch or Florentine Stitch) Bargello uses long, straight stitches, usually over four threads of canvas, to form a definite design. The stitches are worked horizontally or vertically on the canvas to form a rising and falling pattern. To get the up-and-down effect, stitches are raised or lowered two canvas threads at a time. The key line establishes the pattern and is repeated throughout the entire design. Bargello works up quickly, but requires strict attention to the stitching to make each row identical; otherwise, the design is thrown off balance.

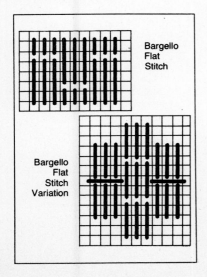

Bargello Flat Stitch

Bargello Flat Stitch Variation

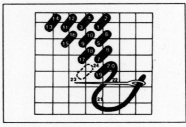

Basket-Weave Stitch

The front of this tent stitch looks like the continental or half cross-stitch, but the back resembles a basket-weave or woven pattern. It is useful for backgrounds and large areas because it does not distort canvas when worked with the grain (see page 9). Begin stitching in the upper right corner and work diagonally, moving the needle vertically on the down rows and horizontally on the up rows. The stitching sequence is indicated by the numbers on the diagram. *(See also, Continental, Half Cross-, and Tent Stitches.)*

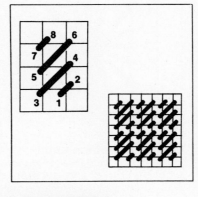

Cashmere Stitch

This stitch, worked in boxes, is made with four stitches per unit. Take the first stitch at the base of the unit and work up. Rows can be worked horizontally, vertically, or diagonally. When used as a background, the cashmere stitch resembles woven fabric. *(See also, Mosaic Stitch.)*

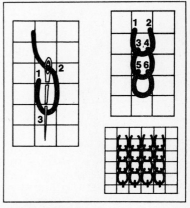

Chain Stitch.

This is a line stitch used for outlining as well as filling. When worked in vertical rows, it resembles knitting. Work from top to bottom over two horizontal threads and between two vertical threads. Pull the needle to the front of the canvas; reinsert in the same mesh and bring up two meshes below. Loop yarn around needle and pull through.

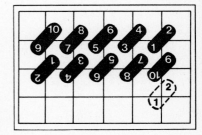

Continental Stitch

The continental stich is a tent stitch good for outlining and filling small areas. (Avoid using it to fill large areas because it distorts the canvas; use the basket-weave stitch instead.) Work from right to left, turning the canvas on alternate rows. Bring the needle up at 1, down at 2, and up again at 3. *(See also, Basket-Weave, Tent, and Half Cross-Stitches.)*

continued

Basic Needlepoint Stitches *(continued)*

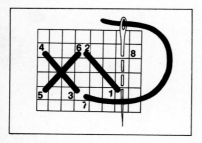

Cross-Stitch

The cross-stitch is made with two stitches — one that slants from lower right to upper left, and one that slants from lower left to upper right. Work in horizontal rows, completing the first half of each stitch and then returning back along the row to cross each stitch. The cross-stitch is a good background stitch; it covers well and you never turn the canvas.

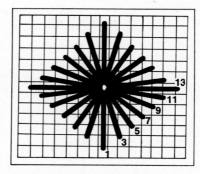

Diamond Eyelet Stitch

(Also called Diagonal Star Stitch) This stitch forms a bold diamond pattern, effective for accenting and highlighting. Work each stitch of the diamond eyelet down through the center hole, pulling snugly to open the mesh. Start at the bottom of the diamond and move counterclockwise, as shown above.

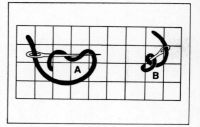

French Knot

The French knot is an accent stitch used for details rather than large areas. When working it, wrap the yarn around the needle only once (wrapping the yarn more than once makes a loose knot). Reinsert the needle into the canvas one mesh away from where it came up. When working a row, go from right to left.

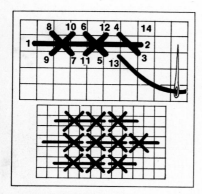

Cross-Stitch Tramé

The cross-stitch tramé is formed with a layer of under-stitching beneath the cross-stitches. Vary the length of the tramé (under-stitches) to avoid a line across the needlepoint. For example, work the tramé stitches over four, six, and then five warp threads. Then cover the under-stitching with cross-stitches. This technique gives full-bodied texture to your work. *(See also, Cross-Stitch.)*

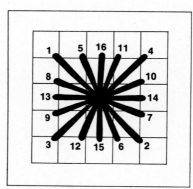

Double Leviathan Stitch

(Also called Leviathan Stitch) A highly textured and decorative box stitch, the double leviathan stitch can be worked singly or in rows. Work a cross-stitch over four horizontal and four vertical threads of canvas. Then cross each arm of the first cross-stitch, making four more stitches as shown. Finally, fill the remaining mesh openings with horizontal and vertical stitches over one thread.

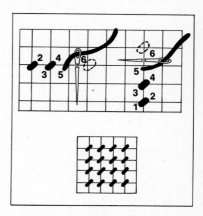

Half Cross-Stitch

(Also called Half Stitch) This is a tent stitch; it is diagonal on the front but straight on the back, and uses yarn more economically than continental or basket-weave stitches. The stitches are thinner and flatter because there is less yarn on the back of the work. Use it only with penelope canvas because it distorts mono canvas. Stitch horizontally from left to right or vertically from bottom to top. *(See also, Tent, Continental, and Basket-Weave Stitches.)*

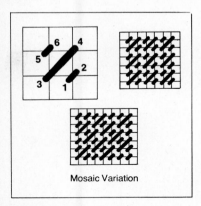

Mosaic Variation

Mosaic Stitch

(Also called Diagonal Hungarian Stitch) This square stitch is made with three stitches. The units are worked one at a time in either horizontal, vertical, or diagonal rows. It resembles the cashmere stitch except that there is one less stitch per unit. The mosaic stitch can be worked in different colors for a checkerboard pattern. *(See also, Cashmere Stitch.)*

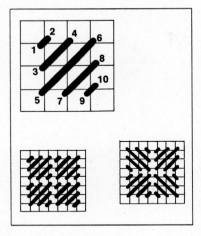

Scotch Stitch

(Also called Diagonal Satin Stitch, Flat Stitch, and Diagonal Flat Stitch) A Scotch stitch is made with either five or seven slanting stitches to form a square unit. It is effective as a border, forming a checkered effect, but distorts canvas when worked over large areas.

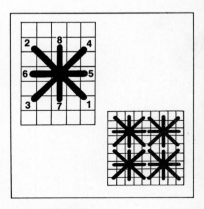

Smyrna Stitch

This starlike stitch is usually used for decorative accents. Work a cross-stitch over two or four canvas threads. Then, cover the first two stitches horizontally and vertically with an upright cross-stitch. When working over two horizontal and vertical threads, the canvas is covered completely, whereas some of the canvas may show when working over four threads. *(See also, Upright Cross-Stitch.)*

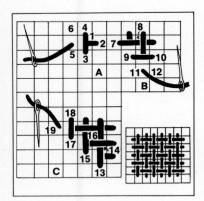

Reverse Basket-Weave Stitch

The woven pattern on the back of the basket-weave stitch appears on the front when working the reverse basket-weave stitch. (Tent stitches appear on the back.) Finish each row with half stitches. *(See also, Basket-Weave Stitch.)*

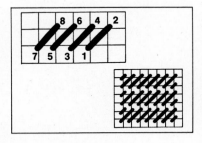

Slanting Gobelin Stitch

(Also called, Oblique or Sloping Gobelin Stitch) This stitch, worked in horizontal or vertical rows, looks like a tent stitch except that it covers two to five horizontal threads of canvas. Take tent stitches at the beginning and end of each row to achieve square corners. This stitch is effective when used for borders and geometric designs. *(See also, Tent Stitch.)*

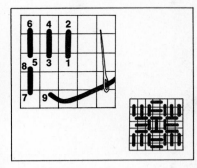

Straight Gobelin Stitch

(Also called, Upright Gobelin Stitch) This is a good border stitch that can be worked horizontally or vertically over two or more canvas threads. Work rows in alternate directions, from right to left and left to right, or from top to bottom and bottom to top. *continued*

Basic Needlepoint Stitches *(continued)*

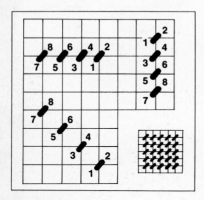

Tent Stitch

"Tent Stitch" is the blanket term used for a slanted stitch that is worked over the intersection of two canvas threads from lower left to upper right, as shown. It can be worked in horizontal, vertical, or diagonal rows. Because it is a small, flat stitch, it is often used for entire designs.

It is only by looking at the back of the needlepoint that tent stitches can be identified as basket-weave, continental, or half cross-stitches. *(See also, Basket-Weave, Continental, and Half Cross-Stitches.)*

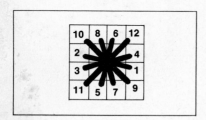

Triple Cross-Stitch

The triple cross-stitch is a square, textured stitch made of three layered cross-stitches. The first one is worked over one horizontal and three vertical threads. The second is worked over three horizontal and one vertical thread. The final cross is made over three horizontal and three vertical threads.

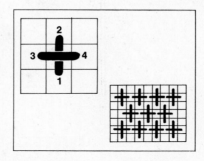

Upright Cross-Stitch

(Also called Straight Cross-Stitch) This textured stitch can be worked singly or in rows. It's a nice background stitch. Make the first stitch a straight Gobelin stitch over two horizontal canvas threads. Then cross the first stitch horizontally so the second stitch covers two vertical threads. For horizontal rows of upright cross-stitches, skip one mesh (two threads) between each vertical stitch. Stagger the position of the crosses from row to row so canvas is covered. *(See also, Straight Gobelin Stitch.)*

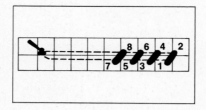

Waste Knot

Instead of tying knots on the back of your canvas, which can cause unsightly bumps, begin and end lengths of yarn with waste knots. Knot the end of the yarn and insert the needle into the fabric from front to back so the knot is on the front side of the canvas. Then stitch over the thread end, securing it so the yarn does not unravel. Clip the knot and pull the end to the back of the fabric.

Designers

Curt Boehringer	28-29
Gary Boling	14-15, 18-20, 30-31
Ruth Colt	64-67
Joan Cravens	10-13
Mary Kay Davis	32-33
Sherry DeLeon	68-69
Judith Gross	70-71
Helen Hayes	78-81
Verna Holt	62-63
Chieko Hoshiai	58-61
Jody House	50-51
Emily Lawrence	24-27
Janet McCaffery	52-54
Margie Poffenbarger	38-39
Gay Ann Rogers	44-45, 46-47
Barbara Sample	24-27
Ruth and Andy Sheidler	40-41
Mimi Shimmin	4-5, 21-23
Ciba Vaughan	48-49, 55-57
Kay Whitcomb	82-87, 88-92
James Williams	72-77
Barbara Darrow Yost	16-17, 34-35, 36-37

Photographers

Mike Dierer	cover, 4-5, 15, 19, 21, 29, 31, 33, 39, 45, 47, 51, 63, 65, 69, 72-73, 89
Thomas E. Hooper	35, 37
William Hopkins	11, 17, 24-25, 40-41, 49, 53, 55, 58-59, 71, 79, 83
Bill Wittkowski	13

Acknowledgments

Blaser/Court Art Studios
Gary Boling
Ruth Colt
Jill Mead
Margie Poffenbarger
Betty Sodawasser